The Great American Log Cabin Quilt Book

The Great American
LOG CAB
QUI

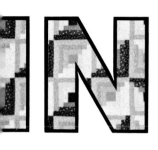

*Complete patterns and instructions for making
all types of Log Cabin quilts*

CAROL ANNE WIEN

E. P. DUTTON, INC.   NEW YORK

Published in the United States by E. P. Dutton, Inc.,
2 Park Avenue, New York, N.Y. 10016

Library of Congress Catalog Card Number: 80-66660

ISBN: 0-525-93205-4 (cloth); ISBN: 0-525-47673-3 (DP)

Published simultaneously in Canada by Fitzhenry & Whiteside Limited, Toronto

W

10 9 8 7 6 5 4 3 2 1

First Edition

Book design by Marilyn Rey

Color insert printed in Japan

To my husband, Leonard, and to our
children, Joshua and Sydney, for
their patience and cooperation

Acknowledgments

A book such as this involves not only the hard work of the author but also the interest and gracious cooperation of many others, whose efforts on behalf of the project I am delighted to acknowledge here.

Special thanks are due my editors Carter Houck and Cyril Nelson for their expertise, thoroughness, and patience; and to Robert Bishop, director of the Museum of American Folk Art, New York City, for his encouragement.

And thanks also to the following whose skills benefited the book in a variety of ways: Beth Bell, Barbara Bracanovich, Leona Casacia, Juan Contijoch, Andrea D'Arias, Nellie Fritz, Cathern Holsinger, Betty Kuntz, Cathy Lenz, Sylvia Myers, Janet Neu, Mary Oakley, Pearl Orebaugh, Harriet Schieser, Karen Searle, Wilma Shaw, Mary Smith, Ruby Stewart, Melba Strecker, Florence Tolson, Linda Webster, Juanita Whitley, and Lynn Zakevich.

Contents

Preface

This book is intended to be a complete reference—for beginners as well as experienced quiltmakers—that simplifies the art of making a Log Cabin quilt.

I have always had a love of color and am fascinated with optical illusions, geometric designs, and intricate patterns. There were no quilts in my grandmother's attic, nor in my mother's. I was dazzled when I first stumbled on an antique quilt, and from that time on I have been consumed with a passion for making my own quilts.

In 1973 I began teaching quilting at the University of Miami School for Continuing Studies in Coral Gables, Florida. The Log Cabin quickly became my favorite design for several reasons. First, the Log Cabin is beautiful, with endless possibilities for design combinations. Depending on how the block units are turned in relation to each other, fascinating things happen to the overall design. Each quilt I make teaches me something new about color, contrast, subtlety, and arrangement.

Second, the Log Cabin can be made quickly and easily in comparison to other types of pieced quilts, which require precisely matched seams. There is no seam matching within the blocks, and minimal seam matching when the blocks are joined to each other. Because all the cut pieces are the same 1½ inches in width with the exception of the center, which is a 2½-inch square, the preparation is simple. Because the concept of the Log Cabin depends basically on an assortment of lights and darks, one can utilize even the smallest scraps of fabric, if desired.

Your final quilt design need not be decided on until many blocks have been pieced. Also, many techniques and shortcuts used in assembling the Log Cabin can be used for other types of pieced quilts.

A fast, assembly-line process can be used to cut and sew the fabric strips. The method is so simple that even a beginning stitcher will get lovely results making an entire quilt top, substituting only patience for experience. Your friends will be astonished by how clever, daring, and well organized you must be. Best of all, you will love the results of your first effort.

When I began teaching the making of Log Cabin quilts, I realized there was much information that should be provided to give the quiltmaker the confidence to begin. How much fabric do you need for all the different designs? What size should the finished top be? How many blocks do you need to make that particular size? How do you begin cutting all those pieces? How do you keep the hundreds of pieces separate from each other? How do you choose your colors? What colors make a striking contrast?

These questions made me realize that I would have to devise a standard block unit that was simple to follow. By making all the finished measurements in 1-inch progressions, I hoped to avoid the confusion that some patterns cause with their more complicated progressions.

A word in praise of simplicity. Being visually oriented, I can usually look at something and understand how it was constructed. However, it is another matter to be able to "read" a pattern successfully. I have a similar problem with a cooking recipe. How can you boil water unless you know what *boil* means? And what do bubbles look like?

Because of my own difficulty in understanding *word* information, I have tried to give definitions and illustrations of any questions and terms that may arise. I have done my best to create a book that would have proved helpful to me when I was a beginning quiltmaker.

I do hope the information in this book will bring you the same hours—and years—of delight that I have experienced. I believe that it will give you an easy, challenging, and fascinating new interest, and that you will soon come to share my enthusiasm for Log Cabin quilts.

CAROL ANNE WIEN

Glossary

BACK   The underside of a quilt, made from a whole piece of fabric, or several seamed together if necessary, and cut slightly larger than the quilt top.

BATTING   A filler, usually cotton or polyester, but sometimes wool, used between the top and the back of the quilt for warmth and loft.

BIAS   The diagonal line on fabric at a 45° angle to both straight grains (the length and the cross). Fabric cut on the bias is pliable and can be stretched or eased to desired shapes. It is, therefore, perfect for use as binding.

BINDING   A narrow strip of fabric, usually bias, but sometimes straight, used to bind or finish edges. On quilts a binding is sometimes made by folding the excess width of the backing over the edge of the top.

BLOCK   One unit of a quilt, usually duplicated many times, then seamed together in a chosen design to form the quilt top. The typical block sizes are 8, 10, 12, 14, or 16 inches.

BORDER   A wide band of fabric, or several narrow bands seamed together, used to frame the finished quilt top.

HEM   The edge of fabric folded and stitched into place to form a clean finish.

KNOT   A loop tied and pulled tight in the end of a thread to prevent the stitching from coming loose. Also, a twist formed accidentally in thread and often preventable by using a shorter thread or by waxing the thread with beeswax.

MARKING   Designs traced on a quilt top as a guide for quilting. A hard lead pencil, a dressmaker's pencil, or a special marking pen (disappearing or washable) is usually used for marking.

MITER   A diagonal seam at the corner of a border or binding, as seen in picture frames.

PATCHWORK   Pieces of fabric seamed together to form a decorative design.

QUILT   A bed covering usually consisting of three layers (top, batting, and backing) secured with quilting stitches. Also used as a verb meaning to stitch together with running stitches.

QUILTING FRAME   A square, rectangular, round, or oval frame, usually made of wood, used for stretching the whole quilt or an area of the quilt while joining the layers with a quilting stitch.

RIGHT SIDE OF FABRIC   The side of the fabric having a noticeably better color, print, and texture. Some solid-color fabrics have no apparent right and wrong side, for example, muslin.

SASH   An interior border surrounding each block in a quilt.

SEAM   The joining or sewing of one piece of fabric to another, usually with right sides together.

SEAM ALLOWANCE   The extra fabric allowed beyond the stitching line on any piece of fabric, varying from ¼ to ⅝ inches in most cases. The allowances in this book are all ¼ inch.

SELVAGE   The finished and reinforced edge on each side of a width of fabric.

SETTING   The arrangement and joining of blocks to form a completed quilt top.

TOP   The upper layer of the quilt, made up of the blocks and sashes, or some other form of decorative pattern.

WRONG SIDE OF FABRIC   The paler and less well finished side of the fabric—the opposite of the right side.

STITCHES:

Backstitch—A stitch in which the needle is run into the fabric from the top, in a straight line under the fabric, and back up. It is then inserted back of the point where it was brought up and another stitch is run underneath—always in a straight line. The stitch that shows on the surface may be very small or you may make it long enough to join the stitch before it, giving the effect of machine stitching. (Fig. 1)

Fig. 1

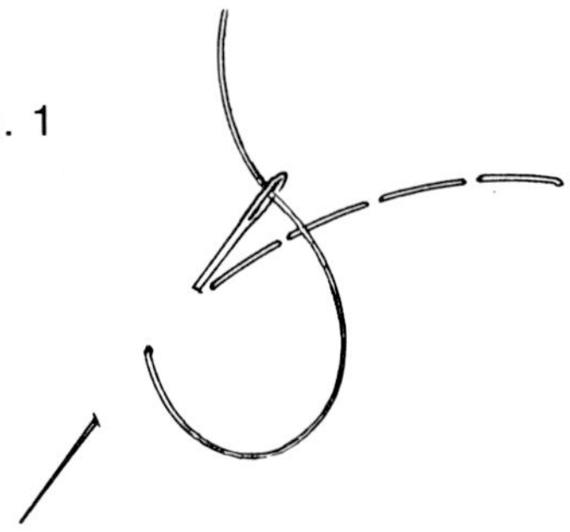

Basting—A long, temporary running stitch used to hold a seam or hem together temporarily, or to hold the layers of a quilt together until the quilting has been completed. (Fig. 2)

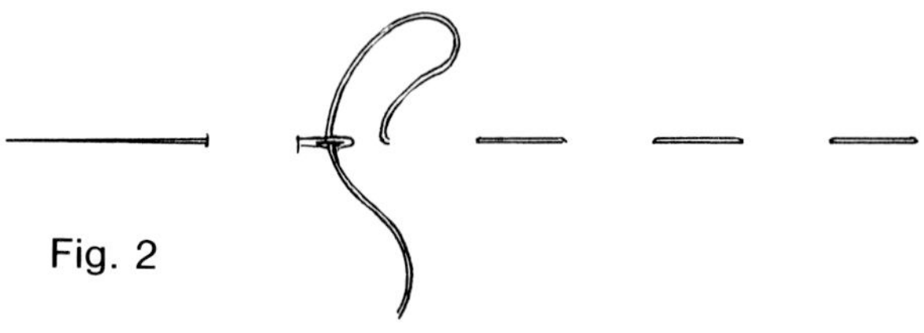

Fig. 2

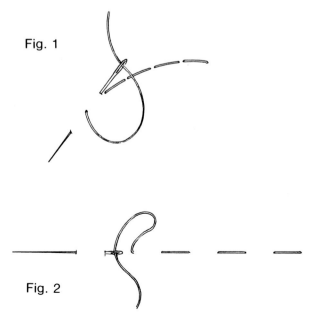

Fig. 1

Fig. 2

Blindstitch—An almost invisible stitch used to hold the turned edges of appliqué and binding in place on the base fabric. The needle is run under the base fabric, up through the turned edge (catching only a thread or two), and then inserted in the base fabric just over the edge from the point where it was brought out. It is then run for less than ¼ inch under the base fabric again and the process is repeated.

Fig. 3

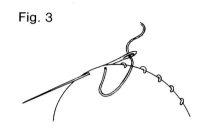

Hemming stitch—Also called *overcast* or *whipping stitch*, this stitch is always worked from the wrong side of the fabric. The needle is brought through the edge of the hem, inserted into the main fabric about ¼ inch along the edge (picking up only a thread or two), and then through the hem edge again at the same time. As this process is repeated, it will leave a row of slanted stitches along the edge of the hem on the wrong side of the main piece.

Fig. 4

Quilting stitch—Small, even running stitches used to hold together the layers of a quilt. They are called quilting stitches, though they may be worked in exactly the same manner as any running stitch. They may also be worked one at a time, straight down through the fabric and straight up again, in which case they are sometimes called *stab stitches*.

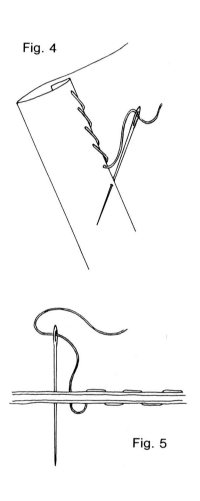

Fig. 5

Running stitch—The most basic of all stitches, the running stitch is worked with a simple in-and-out motion of the needle in a straight line. It may be used to join two pieces of fabric together in a seam, or as a gathering thread, or as a quilting stitch (see above).

Fig. 6

The Great American
Log Cabin Quilt Book

The Great American
Log Cabin Quilt Book

Color

Color is, of course, one of the basic ingredients in making a quilt and in making it beautiful. Choose your colors carefully, always keeping in mind the colors that will touch each other. Most important, for a Log Cabin choose exciting contrasts for the last two long strips that will touch each other at right angles. In other words, the 7½-inch and 8½-inch dark strips and the 6½-inch and 7½-inch light strips will determine a great deal of the impact of your Log Cabin quilt. For a clearer understanding of the discussion that follows, refer to the standard color wheel provided in Plate 1.

PRIMARY COLORS. Red, yellow, and blue are the primary colors. They contain no other colors.

SECONDARY COLORS. Orange, green, and violet are formed by mixing two primary colors that are adjacent to each other on the color wheel:

$$red + yellow = orange$$
$$yellow + blue = green$$
$$blue + red = violet$$

TERTIARY COLORS. Red-orange, yellow-orange, yellow-green, blue-green, blue-violet, and red-violet are formed by mixing a primary color with a secondary color adjacent to it on the color wheel.

COMPLEMENTARY COLORS. Red and green, orange and blue, and yellow and violet are colors that are opposite each other on the color wheel. True complementary colors, when mixed, appear gray. Used together, complementary colors will appear to vibrate slightly, adding visual excitement to your quilt.

ANALOGOUS COLORS. These are the colors that lie adjacent to each other on the color wheel.

WARM COLORS. Red, orange, and yellow are warm and come forward visually.

COOL COLORS. Green, blue, and violet are cool and recede visually.

MONOCHROMATIC. This word is used to describe anything that is all in the same color (hue) in a range of tints (the lights formed by mixing the colors with white) and shades (the darks formed by mixing the colors with black).

CONTRAST. The use of a dark color next to a light one makes a more startling effect or contrast than dark with dark or light with light. Dark colors appear heavier than light ones because the more black in a color, the more it absorbs light; the more white in a color, the more it reflects light.

You may not be striving for contrast in all your quilts. You will want some to be muted and serene; you will want some to be bold and striking. Many times when you are arranging colors, "happy accidents" occur.

Color, shade, and tint add flavor to the room in which your quilt will be used. Play with practice blocks, trying several variations to be sure of the combination you want.

Often a dark color on the light side or a light color on the dark side of a Log Cabin block can work wonders for the subtlety of the color and composition. In the Log Cabin examples drawn for this book, the colors called for are lights, darks, and a bright center. With imagination any of these can be changed effectively at your whim.

Preparing to Make a Quilt

MATERIALS

BATTING—Both polyester and cotton batting are now popular, due to new processes of manufacture that have made them smooth, stable, and easy to work with. For a more antique look you may prefer an all-cotton batting or cotton with 20-percent polyester. The all-polyester batting gives a higher loft, and there is now some extra-thick polyester made especially for comforters. Wool batting is available and very practical in cold climates. It can be split and made thinner for use in more intricate quilting.

CARBON PAPER—Use it to trace patterns onto template material.

CARDBOARD—Good firm cardboard is suitable for use as template material. Ordinary cardboard will not last long, as templates made from it will soon wear away at the edges as you trace around them. Gluing sandpaper to cardboard will both strengthen it and make a good surface that adheres to the fabric.

COLORED PENCILS OR PENS—Use them to make a color mock-up on graph paper in order to determine how the pattern will actually look.

WASH-OUT PENS—These relatively recent inventions can be used on most fabric for marking around templates and even for marking quilting designs on the surface. Read the directions that come with them and test them on scraps of the fabric you are using.

DRESSMAKER'S LIGHT MARKING PENCILS—These pencils will make easy-to-see quilt marking on a dark or busily printed fabric. They can be sharpened to a fine point.

FABRICS—Calicoes, 100-percent cotton, permanent press, polyester blends, broadcloth, chintz, and gingham are the fabrics most used for quilts because they are easy to quilt through and washable. If you plan to use other fabrics, read about press piecing (page 15) and other alternatives (page 94).

GRAPH PAPER—A marvelous aid in designing new patterns and in scaling the pattern of your choice to see the total effect.

MASKING TAPE—Use it to hold together the rows in a quilt top, keeping the sequence straight for seaming.

NEEDLES—Size 7, 8, 9, and 10 needles are the sizes used for all hand work on quilts. The smaller the number, the larger the size, so a #7 will be easier to thread, but most quilters prefer a tiny #9 or #10, which enables them to make smaller stitches. The style of needle preferred by most quilters is a very short "between" or "quilting" needle. For a slightly longer needle, sometimes used in piecing or appliqué, choose "sharps."

PAPER CUTTER—A fast and accurate implement for cutting many layers of fabric on a straight line.

PENCILS—If you use a pencil to mark the quilt top, a #4 or #5 hard lead pencil is recommended, ensuring fainter lines. Be careful to mark lightly so that the quilting stitches can cover the lines.

PLASTIC BAGS—There are many uses for small- and medium-size bags when you are keeping colors, segments, and blocks separated.

RUBBER CEMENT—Use this as a bonding agent to attach a layer of sandpaper to the back of a cardboard template so that it will not slip as you draw around it on the fabric.

RULER—Use a transparent 12-inch ruler divided into ¼-inch markings so that the seam allowance can easily be drawn on the fabric if you do not choose the two-template method of marking. Keep the ruler handy at the sewing machine to check on the accuracy of your stitching.

SANDPAPER—Use sandpaper to make nonskid templates (see Cardboard and Rubber Cement, above).

SCISSORS—Your choice of scissors is wide, but be sure they are sharp, well-balanced, comfortable in your hand, and used only for cutting fabric. The bent-handle shears are preferable for large cutting jobs, such as a quilt.

SEAM RIPPER—Use this handy and relatively safe blade for taking out the mistakes that we all make. When separating seamed fabrics, use the seam ripper to cut through every tenth or twelfth stitch. The seam can then be pulled gently apart along the loosened stitching line. If necessary, use the seam ripper again where the stitches do not pull out easily. Be sure to brush out the cut threads, or they will plague you when you start to restitch the seam.

SHOE BOXES—Another good type of container for quilts in progress. They are free, can be decorated with contact or giftwrap paper, and can be labeled to keep quilt parts separated. Shoe stores throw out boxes daily; you can collect same-size ones that will stack in your bookcase.

STENCIL PLASTIC—A medium-weight, translucent plastic in sheets, available from art stores and some quilting suppliers, easy to cut with household scissors. Use it for long-lasting templates.

STRAIGHT PINS—The ones with colored heads are easy to handle and easy to see, whether on the fabric or on the carpet. If you are accustomed to pinning seams and machine stitching across them, use the almost headless "silk pins."

THREAD—Mercerized cotton thread, size 50 or the stronger size 30, is best for machine sewing. Quilting thread is so designated on the spool and may be used for piecing as well as for quilting.

THREAD NIPPERS—This gadget is held between the thumb and index finger to facilitate faster thread cutting. It is especially useful for separating all the seamed block sections in the "assembly-line" method of machine piecing (see page 15).

TRACING PAPER—There are many uses for tissue tracing paper, such as copying patterns quickly from a friend's supply. It can also be used to keep books and magazines intact when making templates from the printed patterns. Place the tissue tracing paper on top of the pattern page, securing it with masking tape or paper clips. Place the carbon and cardboard under the pattern page in the normal order. Draw the pattern, using a ruler when necessary and a very hard pencil so that the carbon transfer will be made successfully to the cardboard. There will be no mark on the page, and the tissue tracing paper can be removed and kept as a record if you don't own the book or magazine.

YARDSTICK—This is the easiest way to measure fabric as well as to mark a quilt top if a straight-line pattern or grid design is to be used. Some wooden yardsticks are inaccurate and even bent; a plastic or metal one is worth the extra expense.

CHOOSING FABRICS

Choosing your fabrics thoughtfully will determine whether your quilt looks new or mellow with age. If you wish to achieve the look of an older quilt, carefully select prints with designs and colors similar to the fabrics seen in antique quilts. Study the look of the fabrics in the photographs contained in this book, or go to a museum or antiques shop, and note carefully the fabrics that work most successfully. Notice small floral patterns and unusual colors.

Start a fabric collection, choosing a good assortment of your favorites. Make sure you are attracted to those fabrics suitable for a quilt and not for a beach blanket or Halloween costume! You might find it easier at first to keep to miniature and small prints, stripes, or checks because your Log Cabin strips are so narrow that larger prints require more careful cutting and blending.

The wonderful thing about the Log Cabin pattern is that, as long as you keep to the distinction between light and dark, any fabric can be replaced by another when necessary. For example, six months ago you bought your fabric and have finally cut out the quilt. Alas, you need a half-yard more of a dark blue print that is no longer available. You can easily substitute any other dark blue print for the original in the remaining blocks.

Choose fabrics such as calico, broadcloth, cotton, cotton-polyester blends, chintz, and gingham. (See page 94 for suggestions about using silks, wools, and velvets in copying late-19th-century quilts.) There are a few cotton or cotton-blend fabrics, such as sheeting, that are too closely woven and so will be difficult to sew through. Fabrics that are too loosely woven or thin will also cause problems. (See suggestions on page 15 for handling such fabrics.) Try to be somewhat consistent in choosing the fabrics that will be used together. Feel a fabric and test it by draping and folding; then you will know more about how it will react.

Flea markets, garage sales, antique shops, auctions, and your own family's discarded clothes are good places to look for scrap fabric. Remember, *never* use a fabric unless you love it, and *never* use worn-out fabrics that will tear. Buy small quantities of fabrics that appeal to you, regardless of how they look together. When you have a large assortment, you may want to eliminate some to be used at another time. A half-yard here and there will not break your piggy bank, and you will be thrilled at how your well-loved fabrics will blend together to make a marvelous quilt. Don't necessarily close your mind to a certain color scheme. You can use unusual combinations to add excitement and impact to your quilt. It's amazing how beautifully violet can enhance green, and so forth.

FABRIC PREPARATION

Cotton and blend fabrics that are to be used in a washable quilt *must be prewashed.* They may be dipped in warm water until thoroughly wet and then hung up on a straight rod to dry, or put through the washing machine and the drier. (Do not overdry them or they will require real ironing instead of just pressing.) This process takes out the sizing, allows for shrinkage, and freshens fabrics that have been on the shelf or put away for a long time.

If you have any doubt about color fastness in dark fabrics, especially navy, maroon, brown, and black, lay the piece on an old white towel while it is wet to see whether the color bleeds. If the fabric bleeds into another fabric, you have two choices: don't use it, or try to stabilize the color by dipping the piece into a solution of two parts cold water to one part white vinegar, rinsing several times, and testing again.

Fabric is woven with crossing threads, spoken of as grainline. The length grain of the fabric, or warp, runs parallel to the selvage, and has almost no give or stretch. The cross grain of the fabric, or weft, runs perpendicular to the selvage, or across the width of the fabric, and has some give or stretch (Fig. 7). Most fabrics tear somewhat more easily on the cross grain, from selvage to selvage. If the warp is woven with a hard cord thread or rib, the fabric will probably not tear across at all. If you are working with a striped fabric, you may want to cut or tear your strips on the length grain for the design effect. In other words, there are options for using a fabric in one direction or the other when making your Log Cabin strips.

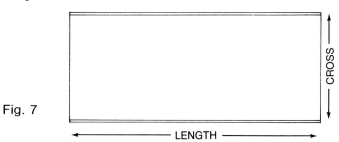

Fig. 7

Before laying out and tearing or cutting the strips, you must straighten the grain of the fabric so that the cross grain and length grain are lying at exact right angles to each other. First, be sure that the ends have been torn or cut along the thread line. Torn fabric will always be straight along the weft or cross grain; it takes great care to cut it that way. Even when the actual thread line is straight, the fabric may look slightly askew. To test, fold the fabric down the center so that the selvages lie together. If one corner at each end lies short (Fig. 8a), you will have to pull those short corners diagonally against each other (Fig. 8b), stretching the fabric until the ends and selvages both lie straight when the piece is folded. If the fabric resists all efforts to straighten it, try pulling it when it is damp. If there is no way to get it reasonably straight, abandon it—perhaps it can be used for appliqué or in some place where grainline is not so important as it is on straight strips.

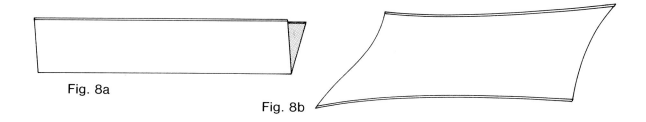

Fig. 8a

Fig. 8b

TEARING OR CUTTING THE STRIPS

The strips for a Log Cabin should be torn or cut on the straight grain (either length or cross) 1½ inches wide. (See above about grainline and tearing). Before you decide whether you should cut or tear the strips, make some tests to determine whether tearing damages the fabric. One-hundred-percent cotton fabrics tear best. Dark prints, and especially cotton-polyester blends, sometimes get a shattered effect for a quarter of an inch or more from the torn edge. Make one tear and then inspect the fabric carefully in a good light to make sure that no pulled threads penetrate deeply into the edge.

If the strips tear evenly, easily, and without damage, you will be able to make all your strips quickly. Snip the selvage at the desired intervals (the chosen strip width—1½ inches), tear across, and snip through the opposite selvage. Always press the torn strips before sewing.

Fabrics that do not tear well must be cut. The cutting lines should be marked with a yardstick and a medium pencil, parallel either to the straightened cut edge or to the selvage. A time-saver, if all the strips are to be cross grain, is cutting fourfold. Be sure your scissors are sharp enough—test to see! Fold the fabric with right sides together down the center so that the selvages lie together (Fig. 9). Press the fold, then fold the fabric again so that the first fold lies along the selvages, then press again (Fig. 10). Draw lines across at the proper intervals, 1½ inches (Fig. 11), as described above. Now pin through the four layers so they don't slide, and cut on the pencil lines. One yard of fabric is about the largest piece you should try to handle.

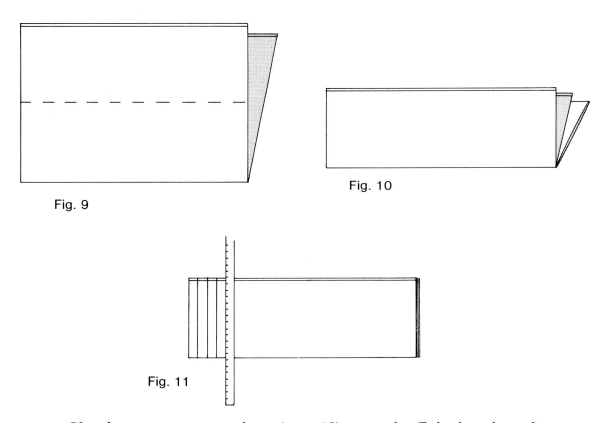

Fig. 9

Fig. 10

Fig. 11

Use the patterns or templates (page 12) to mark off the lengths to be cut from each strip. Be sure that you have read and understood the material on piecing the Log Cabin block (page 14) and have made sample blocks before figuring how many pieces and what lengths of each color you will need.

HALLELUJAH FOR THE PAPER CUTTER

If you want to cut fabric quickly, as I usually do, try a good sharp paper cutter. An 18-inch cutter is large enough to cut with one clean sweep through 45-inch fabric folded in four layers. If your cutter is equipped with a safety bar, remove it, as it will get in the way. One word of warning: always leave the blade down and latched when not in use, and be very careful with your fingers. If you have children in the house, attach a simple padlock to the handle and the frame, and never leave it unlocked for a minute when you are not using it (Fig. 12).

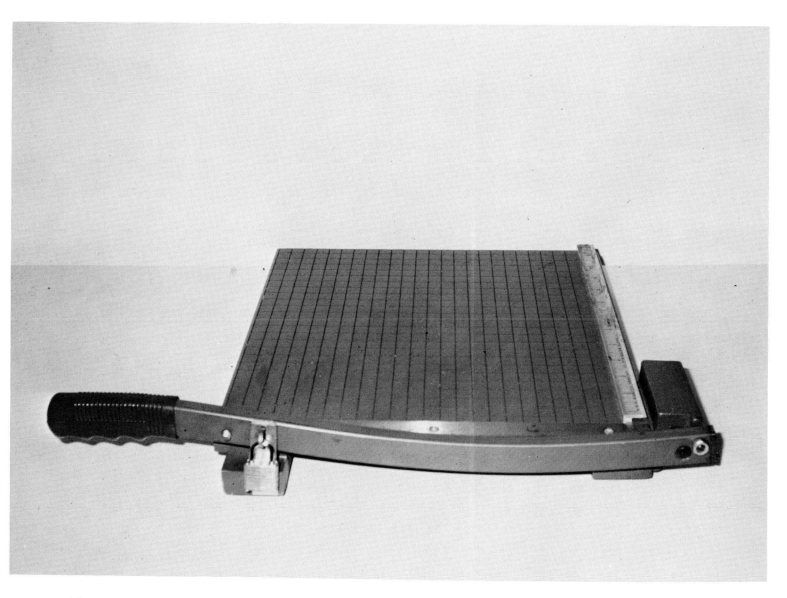

Fig. 12

Most cotton and cotton-blend fabrics can be cut easily on the paper cutter, except those with geometric designs, such as checks and plaids. It is easier to keep those fabrics straight by cutting with scissors, following the thread line in the design. For best results work with a yard or less, just as you would for four-fold cutting by hand. Fold the fabric lengthwise in four layers as described on page 8.

Lay the folded fabric on the table with the carefully straightened end lying along the 1½-inch mark on the paper cutter (Fig. 13). Hold the edge firmly in place, keeping your fingers safely away from the blade. Cut with a firm downward motion, fast enough so that the fabric doesn't pull. Move the fabric over, line it up on the 1½-inch mark, and cut again. If you are using 45-inch-wide fabric, your strips will be 45 by 1½ inches. For the center squares, you will need to cut strips 2½ inches wide.

As you cut the strips, hang them on a rod or a laundry horse, six layers together, so that they are smooth and ready for cutting into the proper lengths on the paper cutter (Fig. 14). Cut off the selvage first (Fig. 15). Mark off the desired lengths on the wrong side of the top layer with a medium pencil, using the templates described in Chapter III, or use the movable guide that screws on the ruler portion of the papercutter, and cut again (Fig. 16). Be sure that you have read and understood the material on piecing the Log Cabin block, and have made sample blocks before figuring how many pieces and what lengths of each color you will need.

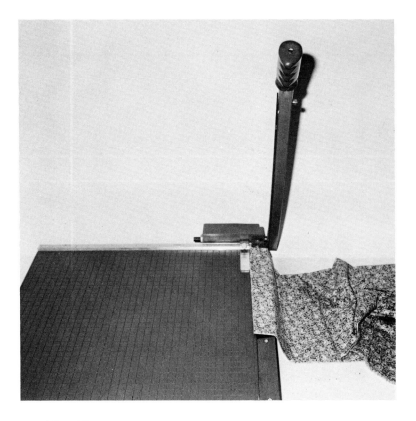

Fig. 13

Fig. 14

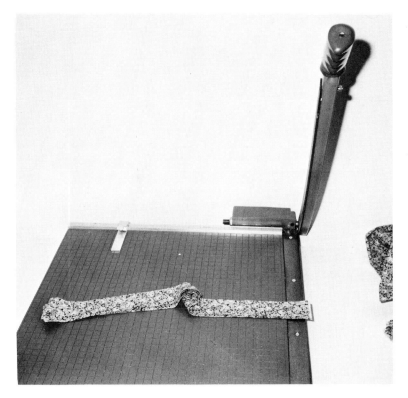

Fig. 15

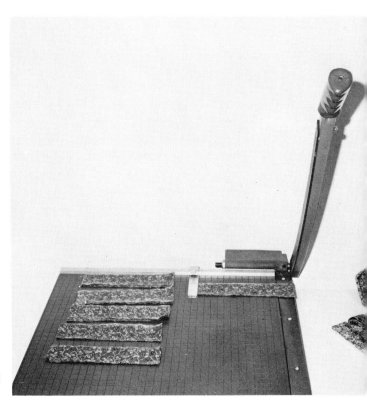

Fig. 16

Making a Log Cabin

PLANNING AND CUTTING THE BLOCKS

The most basic Log Cabin block, the Light and Dark, is a masterpiece of design, full of possibilities for individual interpretation (see Introduction). The elements of the block are surprisingly simple and are kept to one size in this description for further simplicity. Once the technique has been mastered, the widths and number of strips can be changed, the fabrics varied, and the colors used in endless artistic effects. There are many arrangements using the Light and Dark block, with its strong diagonal line, as well as other types of blocks, each with a variety of arrangements. Further chapters will deal in depth with the variations.

The first step for the basic block is to cut cardboard patterns for the center and individual "logs." The second step is to choose the color arrangements from the long strips already cut. Look at pictures of as many Lob Cabin quilts as you can. You will see that some have the colors and fabrics carefully arranged and that others are made up of wonderful scrap pieces, held together only by the use of an arranged light-dark motif. If you are buying fabric and making a planned quilt, you can work with as few as three light and three dark prints and a solid color for the center. The number of prints can be doubled for variety and excitement, as described on page 21. With this one simple Light and Dark block plan, you can make many of the traditional Log Cabin quilts: Sunshine and Shadows, Barn Raising, Straight Furrows, and Streak o' Lightning, to name a few (see Chapter V).

Cut cardboard patterns, or templates, following the diagram on page 12. A firm, hard stencil paper is even better than ordinary cardboard because it holds its shape longer. The patterns, as shown, have the seam allowance included and are the same width as the strips already cut or torn (see page 7).

Piece A will usually be cut from the solid-color strip. The three light colors will be cut as follows: B–C, F–G, and J–K. The dark strips will be cut as follows: D–E, H–I, and L–M.

Lay the template on the wrong side of a long strip of fabric. Mark across the end of the template, move it along, and mark again. It is wise to make four sample blocks to test your color choices before cutting the entire quilt.

There are two ways of making the work of cutting "logs" go faster. In the section on using the paper cutter (page 8), you will find one. If you are cutting

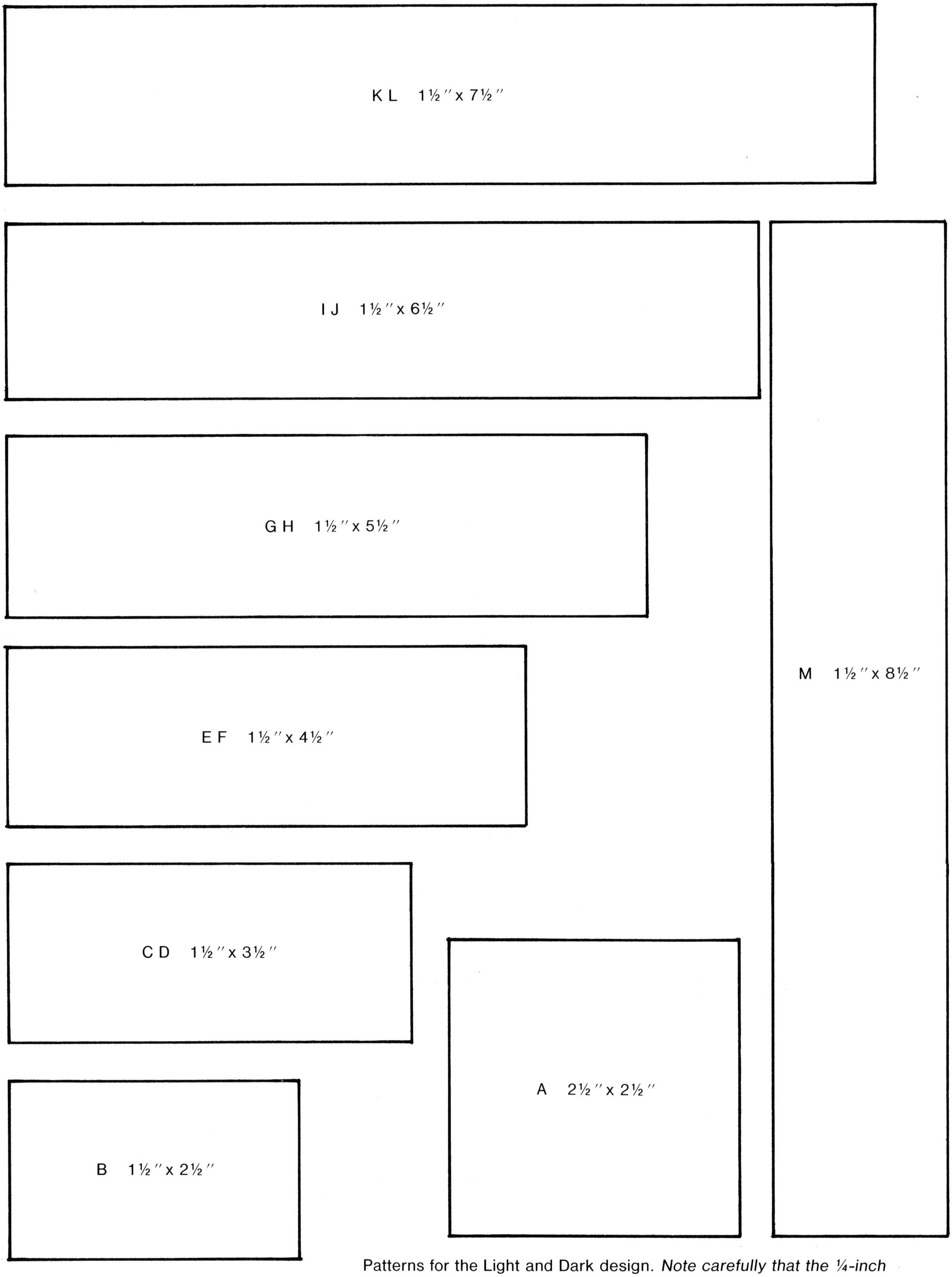

K L   1½″ x 7½″

I J   1½″ x 6½″

G H   1½″ x 5½″

E F   1½″ x 4½″

M   1½″ x 8½″

C D   1½″ x 3½″

A   2½″ x 2½″

B   1½″ x 2½″

Patterns for the Light and Dark design. *Note carefully that the ¼-inch seam allowance has already been included in these patterns.*

by hand, you may be able to cut several layers at a time. Test your scissors to see how easy it will be—six layers is the absolute maximum for most blades. When you know how many layers your scissors can deal with, stack them evenly and pin at intervals (Fig. 17). Mark the lengths with the template and cut.

When you are cutting the pieces for a whole quilt, you will want to keep them separated for easy use: all A pieces together, all B pieces together, and so on. A fine old-fashioned way of doing this is by stringing all like pieces on a strong thread with a knot in one end (Fig. 18). One piece at a time can be pulled off the unknotted end for use as needed. Plastic bags provide another handy way to keep pieces sorted, clean, and easy to see.

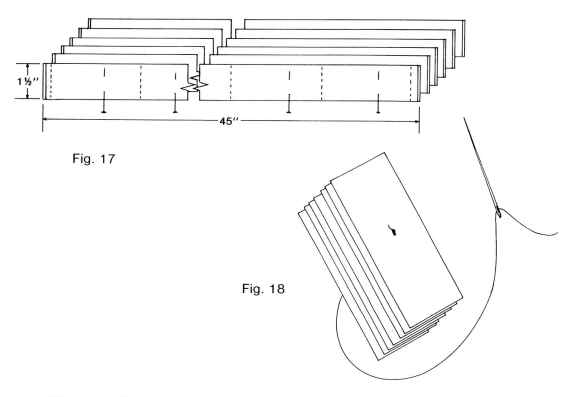

Fig. 17

Fig. 18

You may also want to keep one bag of leftover pieces so that in moments of desperation you can seam together short pieces to make one "log," just as our frugal grandmothers did. Piecing seams should be made on the straight grain of the fabric (Fig. 19).

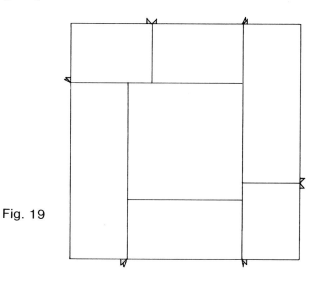

Fig. 19

PIECING THE BASIC LOG CABIN BLOCK

For someone who has never pieced a Log Cabin block, the prospect can be somewhat intimidating. The twelve-step diagrams on page 16 should help—but make a practice block first so that you get the hang of it and are sure your color planning is right. By the time you have finished four sample blocks (page 22), you should find machine-piecing Log Cabins an easy and relaxing way of making a quilt.

Start with the center square and add strips clockwise (turning the block counterclockwise) with a ¼-inch seam allowance, until the block is completed (Figs. 20 and 21). On those first sample blocks you may want to mark the strips A, B, and so on, with pencil on the back. When you have cut enough of them for the whole quilt, you will want to separate the different "logs," as suggested on page 13, marking each group as you put them together on a string or in a bag.

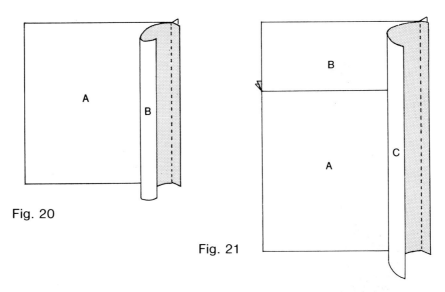

Fig. 20

Fig. 21

I recommend pressing all the seams away from the center. The seam will be stronger than if it were pressed open, the appearance is attractive, and there will be fewer thick seam corners to deal with in quilting.

After you've made sample blocks and are happy with them and with the process, you can go into "assembly-line" production. Line up all the pinned pieces for each step, ready for stitching, and run them through the sewing machine without cutting the thread (Fig. 22 and Fig. 23). When all the B pieces have been joined to all the A pieces, clip the thread that holds the units together (Fig. 24). Press the seams: sometimes finger pressing will do until the entire block is completed and ready for a proper pressing. Line up the A–B pieces with the C pieces to be joined, and stitch them all in another long chain. Clip, press, then join the D pieces, and on and on until you have all the blocks pieced.

14   Fig. 22

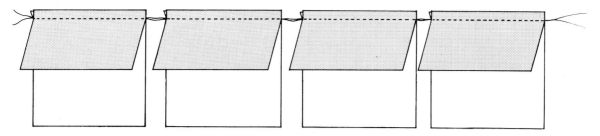

Fig. 23

Fig. 24

There is another way of machine piecing when you are using difficult fabrics—silks, sheers, velvets, and mismatched textures. It is called *press piecing* and employs a base or thin backing block that helps to stabilize the pieces. Use a firm but fairly thin fabric such as muslin, and cut an 8½-inch square. Make diagonal markings from corner to corner to aid in keeping the square even as you add strips to the block (Fig. 25). Lay the A piece wrong side down in the center, pin it in place, then piece as before, stitching through the muslin layer as you seam the pieces together (Fig. 26).

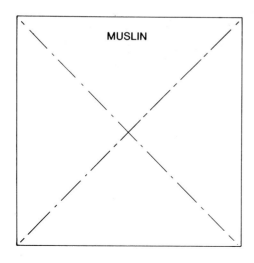

Fig. 25

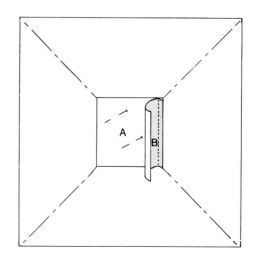

Fig. 26

If the backing is too heavy and some of the fabrics are heavy, quilting may become a problem in press piecing. Quilts of this type are sometimes tied (see page 40) to avoid the extra-layer quilting, or they may be purely decorative pieces, similar to Victorian "throws," in which the batting is omitted, so that the quilting has to be worked only through top, base, and backing.

Light and Dark order of assembly

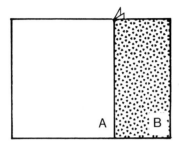

Step 1:
Seam light B to A.

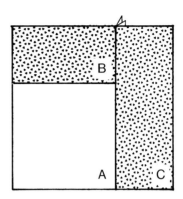

Step 2:
Seam light C to A–B.

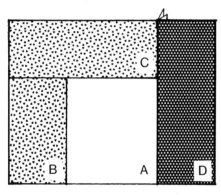

Step 3:
Seam dark D to A–B–C.

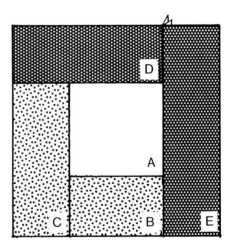

Step 4:
Seam dark E to A–B–C–D.

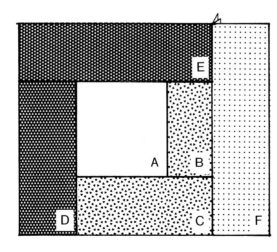

Step 5:
Starting next row, seam light F to B side of first row.

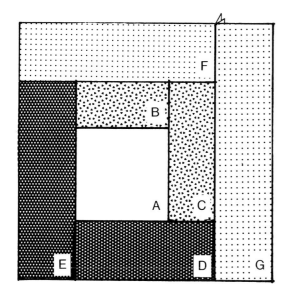

Step 6:
Seam light G to C side
of first row.

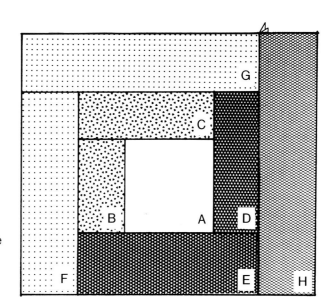

Step 7:
Seam dark H to D side
of first row.

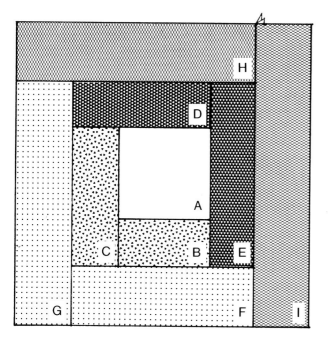

Step 8:
Seam dark I to E side
of first row.

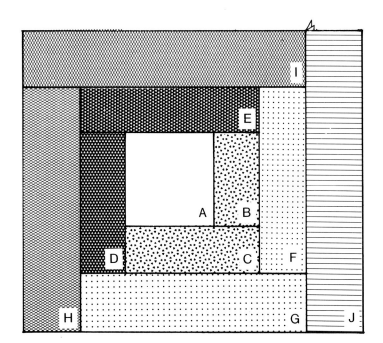

Step 9:
Starting next row, seam light J
to F side of second row.

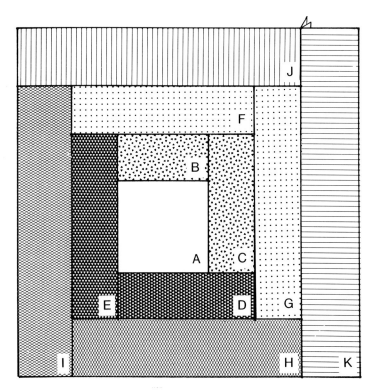

Step 10:
Seam light K to G side
of second row.

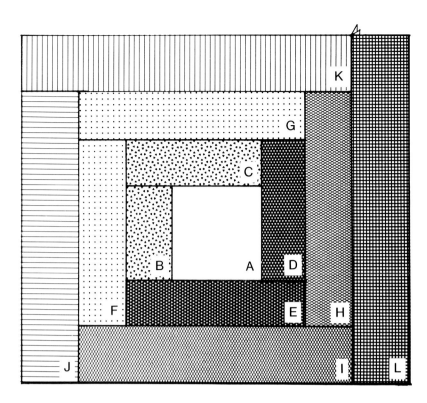

Step 11:
Seam dark L to H side
of second row.

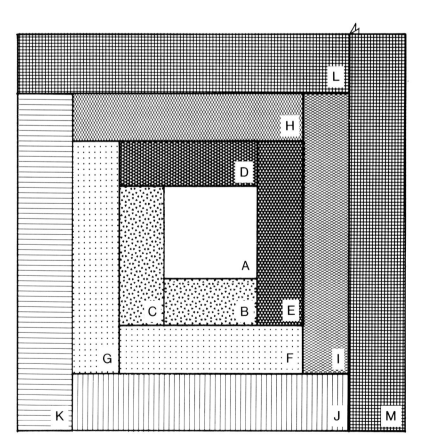

Step 12:
Seam dark M to I side of second row,
completing the block.

Light and Dark (completed)

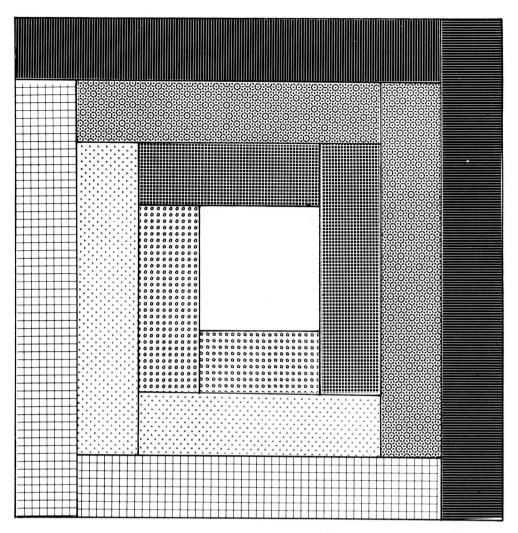

Light and Dark Block #1

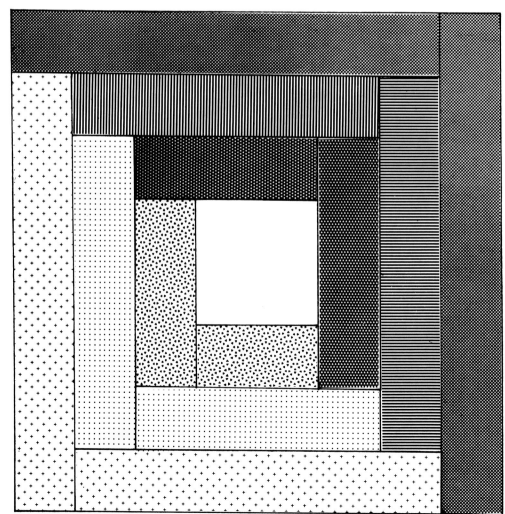

Light and Dark Block #2

USING TWO OR MORE BLOCK ARRANGEMENTS

If you look at block #1 and block #2, you will see that they are identical in every way except for the choice of fabrics. Obviously, you could make a Log Cabin quilt using a block in only one color and fabric sequence (seven different fabrics—three lights, three darks, and a solid color for the center).

My personal preference, however, is to use many varieties of fabric. To me, the charm of the Log Cabin is in the variety of prints, checks, stripes, solids, and so on, that you might choose to include. If you're using scrap fabric, variety comes naturally. I have a more planned version for the quilter who is going to buy a variety of fabrics—calling for the two different blocks. Block #1 uses six varied fabrics, three light and three dark, plus the center. Block #2 uses six varied fabrics, three light and three dark, that are entirely different from those in block #1, plus the same center. For this method you will buy thirteen fabrics.

If block #1 were the only unit used for the entire top, there would be no contrast at the seam joining of adjacent blocks. Instead of having the appearance of a 1-inch strip width where the blocks are joined, you would be stuck with a strip appearing to be 2 inches wide. The same fabrics used on the long outside strip of every block would meet, giving the visual impression of one wide piece. By alternating block #1 with block #2, you will have different fabrics on the edge of each completed block at the meeting point, allowing for the excitement of contrast, not only where dark and light meet (Fig. 27), but also where two darks meet (Fig. 28).

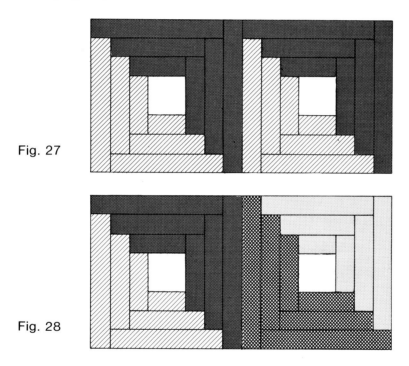

Fig. 27

Fig. 28

Using two different blocks gives the finished top a wider range of sublety and excitement, and you can include more of your favorite fabrics. It is my feeling that you can achieve this by using the simple variation of block #1 and block #2, and yet avoid the confusion of too many choices. If, however, you like experimenting, you can vary the arrangements of those twelve fabrics so that you have more than two distinct blocks.

Now that you have some choices to make, you should put together four sample blocks, two of block #1 and two of block #2, to see how your choice works. When you have block arrangements that please you, use them as a guide for figuring the totals for each fabric.

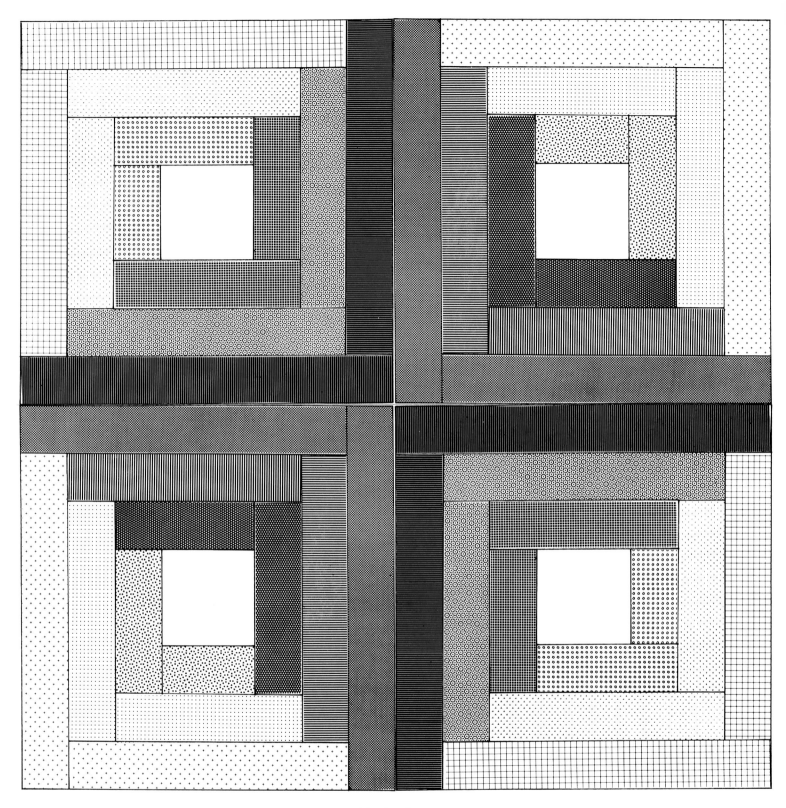

Arrangement Diagram for two #1 and two #2 blocks. In any arrangement
be sure to use the blocks so that "logs" of identical fabric do not touch.

Light and Dark shaded diagram showing the arrangement of the blocks

LIGHT AND DARK ARRANGEMENT

The simplest way to use your Light and Dark blocks is to set four together, two of #1 and two of #2, so that the darks meet to form a diamond, as in the arrangement diagram (page 22). As more sets of four are joined to these, light diamonds will also form, as seen in the overall pattern plan. Six blocks across and eight in length, as shown, will measure 48 by 64 inches. To make a piece in that size you will need twenty-four #1 blocks and twenty-four #2 blocks. The size can be increased in increments of two rows of blocks each way, or 16 inches per increase. Another row of dark diamonds will appear in each direction.

HOW TO FIGURE THE MEASUREMENTS

Now you understand how to make a Log Cabin block, you have chosen your colors, and you have made practice blocks. You are ready to make a quilt or a wall hanging, and you must decide on the finished size of the piece, and how many blocks you will need. You may want to use a simple binding—in exactly the way so many 19th-century Log Cabins were finished—or you may want a border.

Some of your choices are aesthetic and some are practical. Certain arrangements, like Straight Furrows and Wild Goose Chase, look charmingly traditional with only a binding. Some of the more complex arrangements need a border to fill out the dimensions for a large bed. The integrity of the design must be taken into consideration, especially in such bold arrangements as Joshua's Star, which can be made in only one size and changed only with borders. Simpler arrangements, like Birds in Flight and Wild Geese Flying, can be changed by the addition or subtraction of a row of blocks. Barn Raising must be changed in a balanced fashion, adding one row of blocks on each side and at each end. Touching Stars can be changed only in four-block increments. It is necessary to analyze each arrangement before deciding how well it will work in the size you plan to make.

If you are planning a wall hanging, you will be somewhat more limited in the possible number of arrangements that will fit smaller wall spaces and not overpower the room. You may want to experiment with smaller blocks (see Chapter VII). Borders are especially nice on wall hangings, containing the interior design like a frame.

In most cases you will be planning a cover for a specific bed, so of course you must start by considering the dimensions of the bed and the type of bedspread or coverlet that you want. Much of the information for beds can be categorized neatly. A bedspread means a covering that falls to the floor on both sides and at the foot, and that covers the pillows all the way to the headboard, with a few extra inches allowed to tuck under the pillows (Fig. 29). A coverlet is

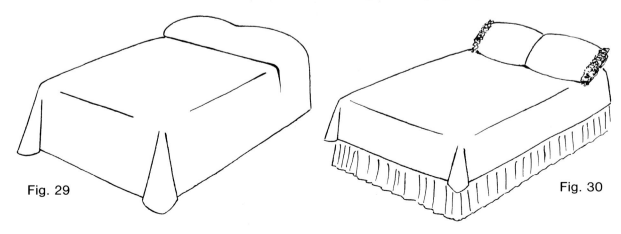

Fig. 29

Fig. 30

smaller, usually falling just over the edge of the mattress to the top of a dust ruffle, and often lying flat under the pillows up to the headboard (Fig. 30).

You can make your own variations on these rules to suit your taste, the particular arrangement you have chosen, and any special needs of the piece of furniture in question. For instance, there are certain problems inherent in four-poster beds and beds with footboards. A quilt is certainly a suitable covering for either of these lovely antiques, but it cannot fall free to the floor at the foot. Our great-grandmothers solved the four-poster problem with their usual ingenuity by leaving out the blocks that form the two lower corners of the quilt (Fig. 31), so that it slipped easily around the posts at the foot of the bed. A border is lost on a bed with a footboard. Actually, any extra length at the bottom is

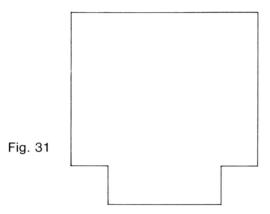

Fig. 31

unnecessary—all that is needed is the amount that will tuck in between the mattress and the footboard.

After taking into consideration all these variations, there are still standard mattress sizes and some rules you can go by. If you can make a plain bedspread or coverlet, without considering footboards and other oddities, you can start with the following measurements.

Standard mattress measurements	Bedspread		Coverlet	
Twin: 39″ × 75″	39	75	39	75
	+44	+44	+26	+13
	83	119	65	88
Double: 54″ × 75″	54	75	54	75
	+44	+44	+26	+13
	98	119	80	88
Queen: 60″ × 80″	60	80	60	80
	+44	+44	+26	+13
	104	124	86	93
King: 80″ × 80″	80	80	80	80
	+44	+44	+26	+13
	124	124	106	93

Bedspreads: Add 22 inches to each side and each end of the mattress measurement, a total of 44 inches to the width and 44 inches to the length.

Coverlets: Add 13 inches to each side and to one end of the mattress measurement, a total of 26 inches to the width and 13 to the length.

There are two other mattress sizes that will surely be of interest to many quilters—the ones for children. Cribs require only about 10 inches extra on each side and 10 inches extra at one end. Coverlets are appropriate for youth beds, so the measurements are as follows:

Standard mattress measurements	Coverlets	
Crib: 27″ × 52″	27	52
	+20	+10
	47	62
Youth bed: 33″ × 66″	33	66
	+26	+13
	59	79

Always remembering that within any of the given charts, rules, and plans, your own preferences must be taken into account, you can start figuring how many blocks you will need in each direction. The block size that you will deal with for any of the basic Log Cabin designs is 8 inches finished. That means, for instance, that you will need ten blocks across and eleven blocks in length for the double bed coverlet, 80 by 88 inches. That's easy! On the double bed spread the division does not work out so perfectly—twelve blocks across and fifteen blocks in length is as close as you can get—giving you 96 by 120 inches. You will probably never miss the 2 inches on the width, and you can save yourself a whole row of piecing by eliminating a row in length. You will then have only 17 inches extra at the upper end to go under and over the pillow—probably ample. Of course, if you use borders, you can change all this even more.

There is really a lot of "fudge factor" all around. The quilting may tighten the measurements and make the finished quilt slightly smaller than you had planned. Your bed may be higher or lower than 22 inches from the top of the mattress to the floor. You may have beautiful embroidered antique pillowcases that you want to display, even on your bedspread, so that you may not want any extra length at the top to go over the pillows. You may not like a border at the top of the bed. Put down all the actual measurements of your bed and then chart several alternatives on graph paper. Even with the best planning you may find that your final decision is made after you have pieced almost enough blocks and laid them out on the floor. Visual changes occur in fabric that were not apparent on paper. You will have to live with a quilt a long time—take time and make sure it is exactly what you want.

Throughout this book you will be working with only four block dimensions when figuring how many blocks to make for any specific quilt. The basic block from which the majority of designs are made is 8 inches square, finished measurement, as mentioned. But when you turn that block diagonally, as for Square Barn Raising, it measures 11¼ inches each way, corner to corner. The same is true for Chevron, another 8-inch block on the diagonal.

Courthouse Steps and White House Steps are both 10 inches square, finished measurement. Pineapple is 14 inches square. All three of these block designs can be arranged in rows of any number without damage to the total effect. The larger the blocks, the less likely you are to achieve the exact measurement on the chart, without using a border, so the Pineapple, at 14 inches square, needs to be "fudged" more. For instance, using Pineapple, the nearest you can come to the 83-by-119-inch measurement of the twin bedspread is 84 by 112 inches (six blocks wide by eight blocks long). By using nine blocks in length, the total measurement jumps to 126 inches long. Even though you can count on the measurements reducing slightly after quilting, the 112-inch length is less unwieldy and probably provides enough length to cover a single pillow on a twin bed.

If you are making a quilt as a wedding present and do not know what size or type the bed will be, you may find that 96 by 112 inches is as near a universal measurement as you can find—for anything over a twin bed. It may or may not go over the pillow, but it will work as either a bedspred or coverlet on any of the three large beds. For the king size it can be turned with the length running across the bed, and not covering the pillow. The measurements for this universal size will vary slightly for the various blocks, unless you choose to use a border. For the 10-inch blocks the total will be 100 by 110 inches. For the 14-inch blocks the total will be 98 by 112 inches. Keep this universal size in mind for raffle quilts or any quilts to be sold.

YARDAGE CHART AND HOW TO USE IT

The wisest thing that can be said about figuring yardage for a quilt is "Always add a little extra." By nature quilters are collectors of scraps and can always use the pieces left over from one quilt as they combine colors and fabrics for the next one. Eventually the answer to all those scraps may be one wonderful random scrap quilt—and what better design for such a combination than a Log Cabin!

You may change the size and alter the arrangement of every quilt design in this book, so it seems best to give a flexible yardage chart that will be useful for figuring by the "log," not by the whole design. The yardage given in the chart is figured with allowance for straightening fabric and cutting off selvages—in other words, not a "tight" measurement. You will always buy for the next highest figure, so if you need sixty of the 4½-by-1½-inch "logs," you will buy ½ yard. You can cut eighty-eight "logs" from that amount, so there will be some left over for that scrap quilt.

It may help you to keep the block diagram with its A–B–C markings close at hand. You may also want to chart your whole quilt top on graph paper and mark #1 and #2 blocks so that you can count the number of "logs" in each size and each color. Paper, pencil, and simple arithmetic should do the rest. Write down the letter and size of each "log" along one side of the paper. Then in the next column write the number of those "logs" needed, both light and dark. In the next column it should be easy to write the amount of fabric for each—¼ yard light, ¼ yard dark, etc.

For instance, in the Courthouse Steps with Alternate Blocks Turned, as shown in the plan on page 80, there will be thirty-five of the 2½-by-2½-inch centers, seventy light 2½-by-1½-inch "logs," and seventy light and seventy dark 4½-by-1½-inch "logs." If you are using the two-block system, eighteen of the blocks will be of one assortment of fabric and seventeen of another, so you must figure thirty-four of one light 2½-by-1½-inch and thirty-six of the other light in the same size. There will be quite a bit of fabric left over in each size, but remember, too much is better than too little!

YARDAGE CHART

Showing the number of "logs" of each size
from specified amounts of fabric

LENGTH WIDTH	¼ YD.	½ YD.	¾ YD.	1 YD.
2½″ × 2½″ [Centers]	48	96	160	208
1½″ × 1½″ [Touching Stars]	168	308	448	616
2½″ × 1½″	96	176	256	352
3½″ × 1½″	72	132	192	264
4½″ × 1½″	48	88	128	176
5½″ × 1½″	48	88	128	176
6½″ × 1½″	36	66	96	132
7⅛″ × 1½″	36	66	96	132
8½″ × 1½″	24	44	64	88
9½″ × 1½″	24	44	64	88
10½″ × 1½″ [White House] [Courthouse Steps]	24	44	64	88

Putting It All Together

MAKING UP THE QUILT TOP

Masking Tape Method:

When the blocks are finished, lay them out on the floor in the chosen arrangement. Use masking tape to hold each row of blocks together (Fig. 32). Stitch the short seams to form rows (Fig. 33). Press all the seams in one direction. On the next row you may press the seams in the opposite direction so that, when the rows are joined, the seams will not form bulk at the meeting points (Fig. 34). Number each row in order with a piece of masking tape attached to the first block.

Pin the first two rows together, being especially careful to see that the corners meet on every block (Fig. 35). If you use large-headed pins, be sure to remove them as you go—they will not feed through the machine without breaking needles. Very fine silk pins can be used to great advantage because they will feed through without damage and hold the rows without slippage. Continue adding rows, one at a time, in numerical order. Press the long seams consistently in one direction.

Shortcut Method:

If you are very careful not to get the blocks out of order, you can work without taping. Lay the blocks out as before, and put the number of each row on masking tape on the first block of the row. Carefully stack the first row in the order in which it is to be sewn and then stitch the blocks together exactly as you picked them up. Press each row as soon as it is stitched. When all rows are ready for the final assembly, lay them out in order on the floor again to make sure you have not sewn any blocks out of sequence. Now you are ready to join the rows, using the numbers taped onto the first blocks as guides.

BORDERS

Borders can be an attractive addition to a quilt, as well as an easy way of justifying the measurements to fit a certain bed. Careful planning of both the border width and the fabric used is necessary to make the border blend in with the quilt and not look like an afterthought.

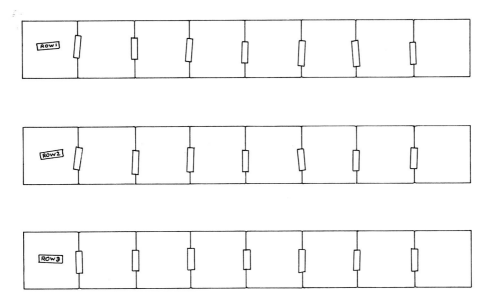

Fig. 32

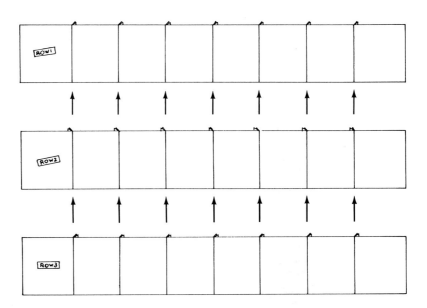

Fig. 33

Fig. 34

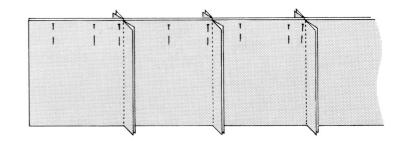

Fig. 35

One way of arriving at a decision is to try the fabrics you have chosen, one at a time, around the four sample blocks (see Chapter III), to see which one makes the best frame. One of the darker fabrics will probably stand out best and enhance the overall appearance most. You can also try solid colors that blend with the prints.

The width of the border is a matter of both artistic and practical choice. If you are using the border to make the quilt the correct size for a bed, you may need only 6 inches, but you may find that 3-inch borders are not especially effective. You then have the option of omitting one row of blocks (8 inches) and using a 7-inch border on each side for a total of 14 inches. You may be able to determine the best proportions from the scaled drawing you have made in the planning stage, or you may want to wait until you have a large number of blocks completed and can lay them out on the floor with the border fabric.

An especially suitable border for a Log Cabin quilt is the strip border, using four of the fabrics from the blocks, usually shading from light out to dark. You may use four even-width strips, from 2 to 4 inches each. An interesting effect can also be achieved with borders of strips in increasing widths, starting with 1½ inches, then 2, 2½, and 3 inches, for instance, for a total of 9 inches (Fig. 36). All these choices take some time and some planning ahead.

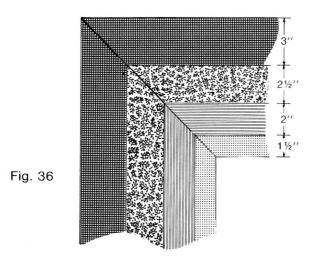

Fig. 36

If you are able to make a decision about the border before buying your fabric, you can buy enough to cut the border lengthwise and avoid piecing. A 4-yard length is adequate for the longest border on any of the quilts in the measurement chart on page 25. Four 10½-inch widths can be cut from 45-inch fabric—the seam allowance brings the width of each to 11 inches, a total of 44 inches, allowing you to cut off the selvages. If you haven't planned ahead for a continuous border, you may cut cross-grain or length-grain sections from the fabric you have and piece them with seams. Do not mix the grains—all pieces must be absolutely straight cross or length grain, but not some of each. If you are using a print, try to match the design so the piecing won't show.

When you plan the borders, you will have to take into account not only the measured size of the pieced quilt top but also the extra length necessary to extend beyond the corners. You will have to add a seam allowance to all measurements, both width and length. There are two border styles to choose from (Figs. 37 and 38). For the standard border (Fig. 37), you will need to add the chosen border width to each end of the border length on two sides only. For the mitered border (Fig. 38), you will need to add the chosen border width to each end of all four borders.

The strip border is so much more effective with mitered corners (Fig. 38) that it should always be planned for that treatment. Seam the strips together, press all the seams in one direction, and handle the borders exactly as you would the one-piece ones.

You may also choose to omit the border from the upper end of the quilt, so that the Log Cabin blocks come all the way up under or over the pillow. In this case you may use the standard treatment or the mitered corners at the bottom end of the quilt.

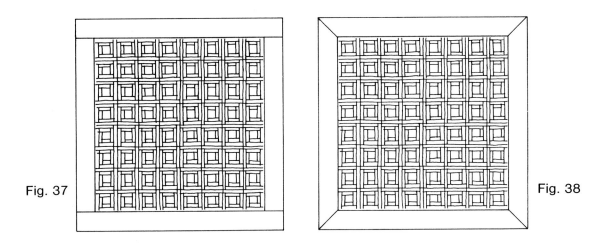

Fig. 37   Fig. 38

CUTTING AND PIECING BORDERS

Before cutting or tearing the strips for a quilt border, reread the information in Chapter II. If you plan to make continuous strips on the length grain of the fabric, you may cut multiple layers by folding once across the center (Fig. 39), then again (Fig. 40), pinning, marking with a ruler, and using good sharp scissors. You may fold once more (Fig. 41) and use the paper cutter (see Chapter II).

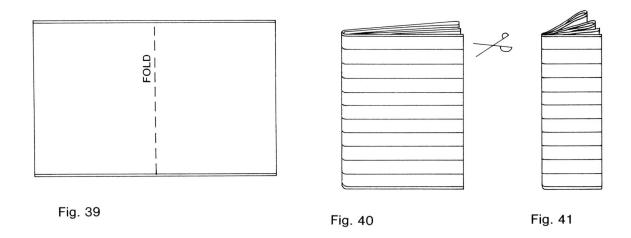

FOLD

Fig. 39

Fig. 40   Fig. 41

Plan carefully if you must piece the border. Have as few seams as possible and try to match print fabrics at the joining. Press the piecing seams open flat to make them less conspicuous (Fig. 42). If you are planning a strip border and must piece the strips, you will want the piecing seams to match all the way across the border (Fig. 43).

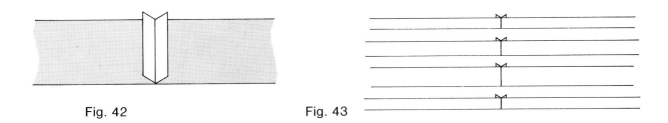

Fig. 42   Fig. 43

Standard Border (*Fig. 37*):

Cut two border pieces to the measurement of the longer sides of the pieced quilt top, without any addition to the length. Cut the other two border pieces to the measurement of the short sides with the planned width measurement added to each end. If you are planning a 6-inch border, you will add a total of 12 inches to the border length for the two short sides of the quilt. Example: For a pieced area measuring 72 by 64 inches, cut two border pieces 72 by 6 inches plus seam allowance, and two more border pieces 76 by 6 inches plus seam allowance.

Pin the first border pieces right sides together with the long edges of the quilt top, matching ends and centers exactly. Stitch the seams and press them toward the border. Pin the other two border pieces in place, matching centers and ends exactly. Stitch and press as before.

Mitered Border (*Fig. 38*):

Add the planned border width to each end of both measurements of the pieced quilt top. Example: For a pieced area measuring 64 by 72 inches, and a planned border width of 6 inches, cut two border pieces 76 by 6 inches and two border pieces 84 by 6 inches, plus seam allowance.

At the end of each border piece, draw a 6-inch square on the wrong side of the fabric, inside the seam allowance. Draw a cross from corner to corner of the square (Fig. 44). Pin the border pieces in place, right sides together with the quilt edges. Match the centers and the ends so that the penciled square extends just beyond the corner of the quilt. Stitch the four long seams only up to the penciled corner squares, and then backstitch to hold the corners firmly. At each corner you will now be able to match two of the diagonal lines to form a perfect miter. Pin the border pieces together along the diagonal lines. If you are making a strip border, be sure that all the seams meet. Stitch along the diagonal line from the inner corner to the outer one, backstitching at the end nearest the body of the quilt for added strength (Fig. 44). Trim away the excess triangle (Fig. 45) and press the seam open flat at each corner (Fig. 46).

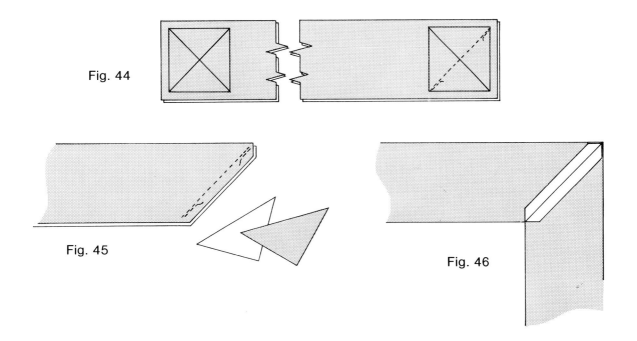

Fig. 44

Fig. 45

Fig. 46

Mitered Border, Hand-Finished Method (Fig. 47):

You may prefer to work from the right side of the quilt so that you can see the miter as it falls into place, especially if you are working with a strip border. You can follow the rules for the first miter up to the point where all four border pieces are stitched into place but the corner squares are still free. With the quilt right side up on a flat surface, fold the corner miter and pin it in place. Use a very fine blindstitch and matching thread to stitch each corner miter on the right side of the fabric (Fig. 47). Trim away the excess triangle and press the seam—it will automatically lie to one side and cannot be pressed open flat.

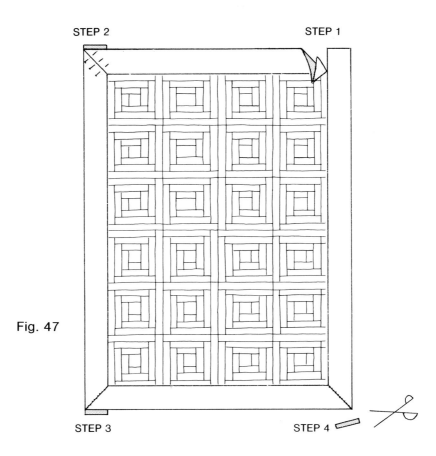

Fig. 47

BACKING AND QUILTING THE LOG CABIN

Log Cabin quilts, in general, are not elaborately quilted. The old-fashioned utility ones were frequently tied at intervals so that they could be finished quickly and so that thicker batting could be used. As quilts have become more decorative and less utilitarian, quilters have become more inventive in their use of fine quilting. Some very adventurous quilters may even use bold, all-over curved designs on contemporary Log Cabin quilts, but this calls for a careful choice of fabrics and a deft hand to manage all those seam intersections. In other words, there is a wide variety of possibilities, and you can make a choice based on the amount of time you want to spend and the effect you want to achieve.

No matter what your choice of quilting style, you must layer and baste the quilt properly first. When all the blocks are joined and the border sewn into place, give the entire top a final pressing. Measure the finished length and width. The backing should measure at least 6 inches more than the top in each direction, and the batting at least 4 inches more.

It may be necessary to piece both the batting and the backing. If the quilt is less than 84 inches wide, two panels of 45-inch fabric can be used for the backing (Fig. 48). The selvage can be left on along the piecing seam only if it is clipped at intervals of 3 to 4 inches so that it cannot shrink and pull the quilt out of shape. If width is not a problem, then trim the selvage away entirely. On a very large quilt you may find that running the fabric panels crosswise makes a better distribution of the seams (Fig. 49). Try to buy batting large enough to avoid piecing, but if this is not possible, cut the necessary pieces and latch them together with the edges butted, using a loose overcast stitch (Fig. 50).

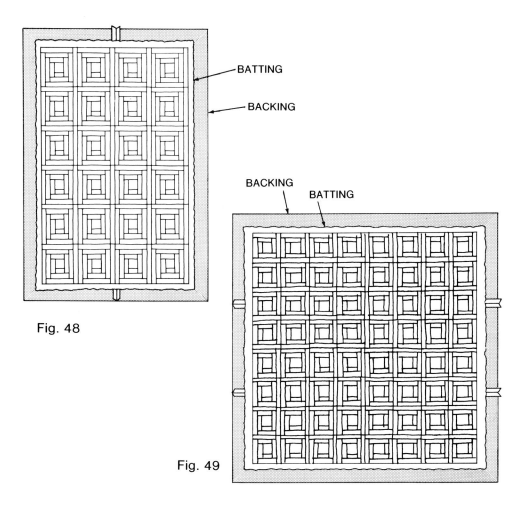

Fig. 48

Fig. 49

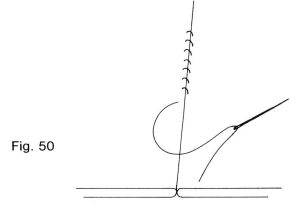

Fig. 50

It is possible to handle the whole layering process without a frame, but in the case of a large quilt, stretching on a frame can make the job easier and give the quilt that wonderfully professional, smooth, taut appearance. If you are fortunate enough to have ample space for a standing ratchet frame on which the quilt can be rolled as you quilt, that can be the best way of all (Fig. 51). In this day of small apartments and frequent travel, lap quilting has, for many people, replaced the frame.

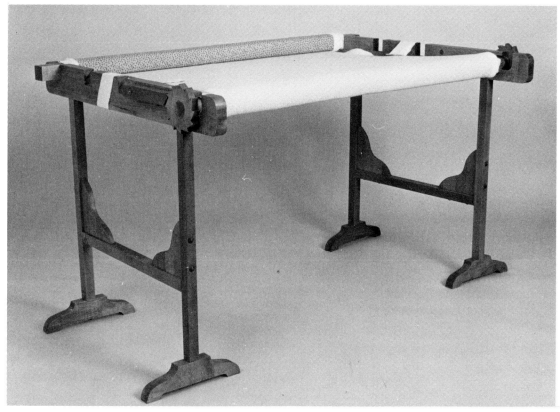

Fig. 51

Photograph courtesy of the manufacturer, Hapco Products, Columbia, Missouri.

If you are making your first quilt, you may find the quilting more bewildering than the piecing, and you will certainly find that there are many more recommended methods. Try to talk to as many people as possible whose quilts you admire—go to the nearest quilt shop and ask questions about the batting, frames, hoops, and anything that puzzles you. Read the directions that come with hoops and frames, and read other books.

Ruth Finley, in her classic book *Old Patchwork Quilts* (1929), describes the original frames used in early American houses as "the four stout sticks." She also explains in some detail that it is very necessary to pull all three layers as tight and even as possible between these sticks and to secure them so that there will be no variation in the tension as you quilt. She also suggests quilting the borders first. Almost anyone today will tell you that starting with the center prevents the problems of slipping and puckering. There is no right or wrong method; it is only a matter of preference. Carrie Hall and Rose Kretsinger, in their 1935 book *The Romance of the Patchwork Quilt*, quite simply suggest sending the top out to a professional quilter, a method much used in the early part of the 20th century, and still possible today.

From all the wonderful information you can get, you must still sort out that which works best for you. As you go along, from the first quilt to the next one, you will decide on methods of your own that may be combinations of several other methods. The result you strive for is a well-stretched quilt with even stitches and straight edges.

A small-to-medium-size piece can be laid out flat on a table or the floor, starting with the backing, right side down, then the batting, carefully centered, and last the top, right side up. Pin the layers together from the center out, just enough to prevent slipping. Baste from the center out to the corners, and straight to all sides, and as many more lines in between as seem necessary, depending on the size of the quilt (Fig. 52). You may want to baste around the edges to keep them straight. You can now use a hoop (Fig. 53) or, with enough basting, you can lap quilt without any type of frame.

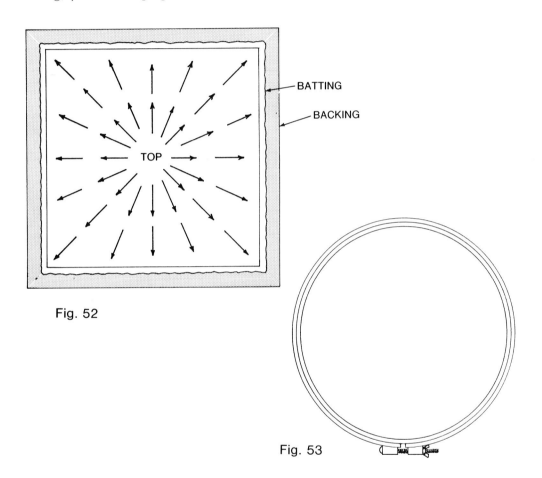

Fig. 52

Fig. 53

If you are making a large quilt, you will find it far easier to stretch it in a standing frame before basting. Each rail of the frame should have strong fabric strips tacked along it. The backing must be stretched very tight and basted firmly to these strips. Smooth the batting out on top of the backing. Lay the finished top, right side up, on the batting. The sides should line up with the side rails and the ends should be ready to roll absolutely straight on the end rails (Fig. 54).

It is also advisable to see a demonstration by someone who has perfected a method of stretching and basting or pinning on a large frame. There are many little tricks that can be explained only by demonstration, but the basic principle is to keep the layers taut as you go. You may roll both ends and baste from the center, or you may roll one end only and baste from that end.

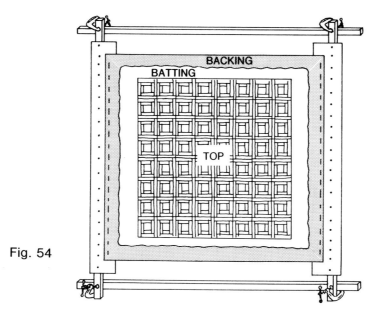

Fig. 54

Many people pin-baste all over the quilt (usually using small gold safety pins to prevent snagging and scratching) and then remove the quilt from the frame for lap quilting, either with or without a hoop. If more than one person is going to quilt, it is necessary to leave the quilt in the frame. There is something very appealing about a quilt set up in a frame, and there is certainly less wear and tear on it than there is when it is moved around.

The quilting stitch is a simple running stitch (see page xv) worked through all layers with a single thread of manageable length. Some people work one stitch at a time, straight down, then straight up through the fabric (Fig. 55), but this is neither necessary nor the only way to achieve perfectly even stitches of the size you want. With a little practice it is possible to run several stitches, small and even, along the needle, before removing it from the fabric (Fig. 56). For most people this produces a better stitch, especially on the back of the fabric, without years of practice, than the one-at-a-time method known as stab-stitching.

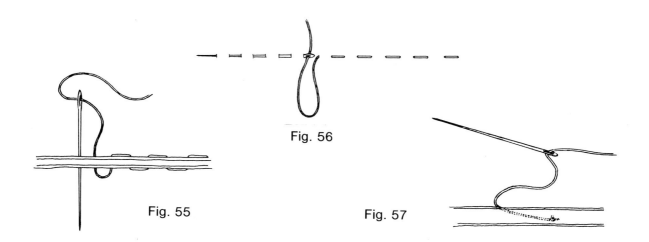

Fig. 56

Fig. 55

Fig. 57

Tie a small, neat knot in the end of the thread. Run the needle through the backing and the other quilt layers on a slant until it comes out on the top where you want to start your stitches (Fig. 57). Give the thread a quick tug until you hear the knot pop through the backing into the batting, where it should lodge securely. At the end of the stitching fasten the thread with a tiny backstitch, worked into the last stitch so as to be nearly invisible. Run the thread between the layers as far as the needle will go again and out on the backing. Cut the thread close so that the end disappears inside. The subsequent rows of quilting should secure the threads between the layers so that no more fastening is necessary.

At points where the stitches cross over the seams, it is more difficult to keep them even. Because all the seams have been pressed outward, it is best to work a row of quilting about ⅛ to ¼ inch inside each seamline on Log Cabin designs (Fig. 58). Another method, especially good on heavy, unmanageable fabrics, is called "stitch in the ditch." All the stitches are directly in the seamline and nearly invisible. The final effect is much like the One Block at a Time method in Chapter VIII.

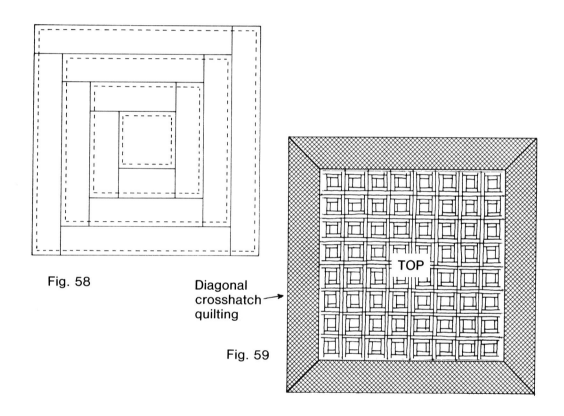

Fig. 58

Diagonal crosshatch quilting

Fig. 59

Only in the center square of each block and along the border of Log Cabin quilts can intricate quilting patterns be used effectively. Tiny leaf or flower designs are suitable to the small center squares. Any border design may be used, but the simplest and most usual one is the diagonal crosshatch, with the rows an inch or less apart (Fig. 59). Many quilting designs are available on pattern sheets or in books. They can be traced onto the fabric with special wash-out pens or pencils made for this purpose. Place the paper pattern on a light box, the fabric right side up on top of the paper, and then trace, using a light color on dark fabric and a dark color on light.

Very adventurous quilters may use bold, curved, all-over designs on Log Cabin quilts, especially the more contemporary ones. It is necessary to use fine fabrics that are easy to stitch through and to be a dedicated and proficient quilter to be able to deal with all the seam intersections encountered in this type of quilting.

Tying is the good old-fashioned alternative to quilting a Log Cabin quilt, especially when a heavy batting is used. Fine acrylic yarn in a matching color is suitable in appearance, washable, and relatively strong. Use a sharp long-eyed needle (embroidery style) large enough to hold the yarn. Prepare the three layers of the quilt as before so that they will not slip during the tying process.

On tied quilts the ends of the threads are usually left on top as decoration, but if you prefer, you can tie on the wrong side and cut the threads off shorter. Depending on your decision, you will start on the top or the backing side of the quilt, taking a ¼-inch stitch, usually through the corner of the block. Take one more stitch in the same holes and then tie the ends together in a square knot, leaving short ends of thread showing (Fig. 60). Sometimes small bow knots are used for a more decorative effect.

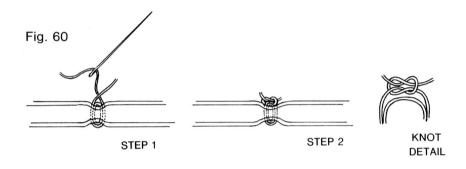

Fig. 60

STEP 1   STEP 2   KNOT DETAIL

FINISHING THE QUILT

After all the hours of planning and work that go into a quilt, the temptation to hurry through the finishing can be almost irresistible, but resist it you must! There are three common ways of finishing, each with several variations. You must think them through to decide which is best suited to your fabric and design. A short discussion of the methods may be useful in giving you some idea of the advantages and problems of each.

The most popular form of finishing the quilt edge is the fabric binding. It may match the backing or any fabric in the top, or a new fabric may be introduced as a sharp contrast. Single-layer binding may be cut either on the straight grain or on the bias. Some fabrics—and especially prints—may show to better advantage one way and some the other. The choice may depend on the way the fabrics handle or on personal preference. Double or French bias binding is long wearing and attractive but cannot be made of very thick fabric.

There are two methods of finishing an edge without a binding. The one most favored by quilters of the last century is the backing folded over to look like a binding. The last, and probably least attractive, method of finishing a quilt is to turn the edges of both the top and the backing and blindstitch them together; this method is more suited to a comforter than to a real quilt.

Binding:

The assembled and quilted piece must be trimmed evenly along the edges (Fig. 61). Then you may figure the length of the binding by measuring across the length and width at the center of the quilt (Fig. 62). You will find that the quilt has tightened up in the process of quilting and that the measurements are slightly shorter than your original estimate. It is that difference that may make a bound edge ripple if the binding is cut to the original measurements. The slightly shorter binding acts as a stay, holding the edges to the size of the quilt laid flat. When making the final estimate for the binding length, allow an extra inch at each corner for the miters and some extra at the end for joining.

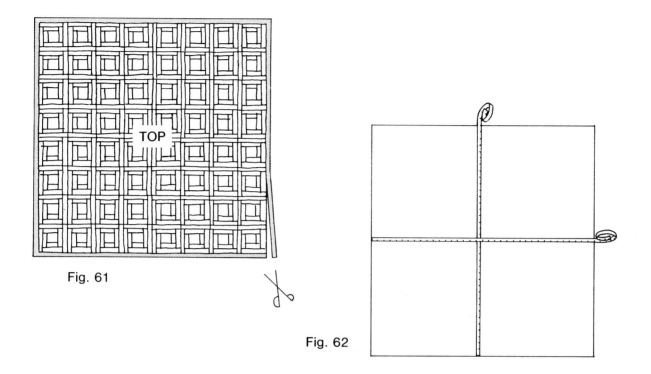

Fig. 61

Fig. 62

The binding should be cut and pieced to make a continuous strip. Straight binding handles a little more easily when cut cross grain, but there is such an obvious advantage to the longer strips of the length grain that you will probably prefer to cut that way. Never use mixed length and cross grains—even the color will look different. Always measure and mark the pieces to keep them on grain (Fig. 63) and seam them together on the opposite grain. Straight binding must be cut almost five times the finished width (2⅜ inches of cut binding will finish to about ½ inch).

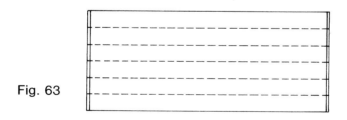

Fig. 63

Bias binding must be cut on the true bias. Fold the fabric so that the length grain lies on the cross grain and the fold will be on the true bias (Fig. 64). Mark this line and then mark the strip widths parallel to the first line (Fig. 65). The width of the bias binding strips should be slightly more than four times the finished width (2¼ inches of cut binding will finish to about ½ inch). All strips should be cut in the same direction, and all ends should be on the same grain— either length or cross—for piecing. Lay the straight ends of two pieces right sides together and pin so that a notch is formed on each edge ¼ inch from the cut end (Fig. 66). Stitch directly from notch to notch (Fig. 67), taking a ¼-inch seam.

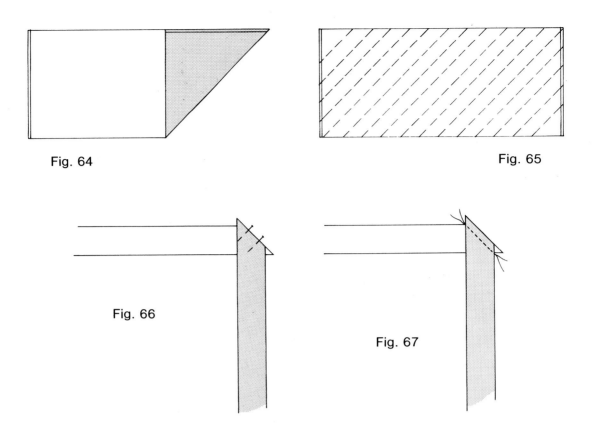

Fig. 64

Fig. 65

Fig. 66

Fig. 67

Starting at the center of either end or side of the quilt, pin the binding right side down on the top, matching the raw edges (Fig. 68). Hold the quilt edge in to the binding so that the finished piece will lie flat with all edges conforming to the measurement taken across the centers. Allow slightly less than one fourth of the total width of the binding for the seam, and continue pinning along the seamline. At the corner stop exactly one seam width before the next raw edge. Turn the binding around to lie along the next edge, allowing a pleat to form in the corner (Fig. 69). The miter is made with this extra fabric. Pin along the next side, always keeping in mind the cross-center measurements.

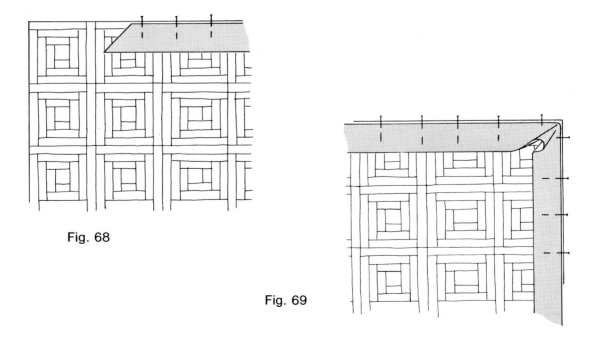

Fig. 68

Fig. 69

42

Stitch along each side, remembering to keep the seam width a scant one fourth of the total binding width. At each corner pleat, stop and backstitch. Fold the pleat out of the way as you start along the next edge, backstitch again, and continue along the next side. On the back of the quilt the two backstitched points should meet in a true corner (Fig. 70a and b). Join the ends of the binding together with a small seam before stitching the final edge of the binding into place.

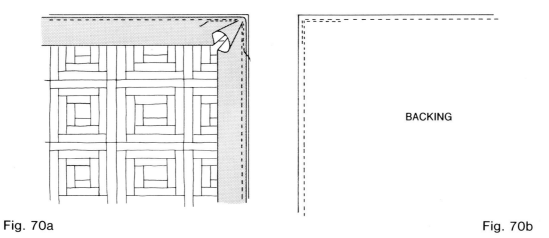

Fig. 70a

BACKING

Fig. 70b

Turn the binding over the edge smoothly. Turn the outer edge under and lay it against the stitching line on the back. Pin the turned edge in place (Fig. 71). Miter each corner by working the pleat into a diagonal line so that the corner is not rounded or puckered (Fig. 72). Finish the binding against the backing with a blindstitch.

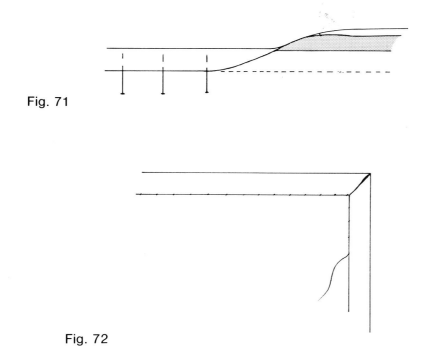

Fig. 71

Fig. 72

For double or French bias binding, the strip should be cut a little more than six times the finished width (1⅝ inches will make a ¼-inch finished binding). Fold the strip wrong sides together along the center and press gently without stretching. Lay the raw edges against the raw edge of the quilt top, and pin as in the first method, leaving pleats at the corners. Stitch all the layers together, taking a seam of slightly less than one third the folded binding width (Fig. 73). Turn the double binding over the edge and finish the folded edge against the stitching line as on the single binding.

Fig. 73

Fold-over Backing:

To finish the edge with the backing, start by trimming only the top and the batting. Mark the backing for trimming so that it extends beyond the top and batting twice the planned finished width (1 inch for a ½-inch binding, for instance), and trim. Fold the corners across at the edge of the top and batting to form a triangle (Fig. 74). Trim off part of the triangle, leaving a ½-inch seam allowance folded (Fig. 75). Fold the sides in half so that the raw edges of the backing touch the other raw edges (Fig. 76). Fold the edges over again so that they completely cover the top and batting, making a smooth, firm edge almost like the bound ones. Pin the edge in place and finish with a very fine invisible blindstitch. Blindstitch the mitered corners (Fig. 77).

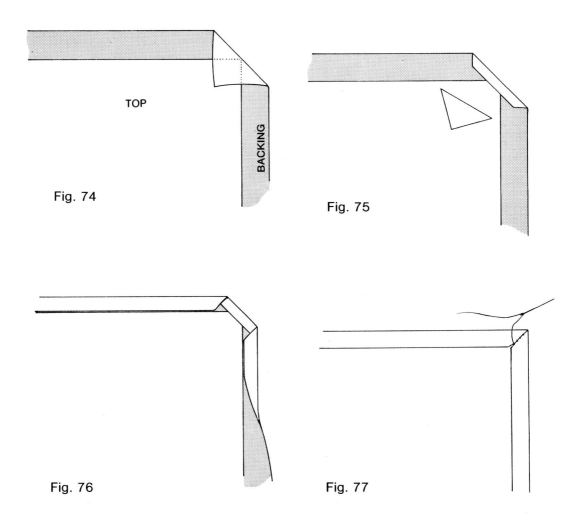

TOP

BACKING

Fig. 74

Fig. 75

Fig. 76

Fig. 77

Turned Edges:

Trim the batting neatly so that it is at least ¼ inch shorter than the top. Trim the backing even with the top. Fold the edges of both the top and the backing so that all raw edges are inside and so that they cover the batting (Fig. 78). Use a blindstitch or a running stitch worked in and out between the folded edges—this last is sometimes called a slipstitch (Fig. 79).

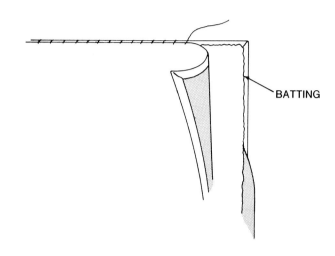

BATTING

Fig. 78

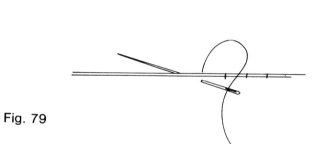

Fig. 79

V

Other Wonders from the Basic Pattern

OTHER ARRANGEMENTS AND PATTERNS FOR LIGHT AND DARK BLOCKS

The designs that can be made from the basic Light and Dark blocks are almost endless. The following pages show some examples of the possibilities—with graph paper and a pencil you can make up many others. Though the effect of most of the designs is strongly diagonal, the blocks are set square to the edges of the quilt. The exception to this is Square Barn Raising, which is shown with its special instructions at the end.

With two exceptions, the patterns will be more pleasing when made with the #1 and #2 blocks. Some designs can be increased in size by adding one or more rows to sides and ends, as you choose. Others must have two or four rows added so that they do not lose their symmetry. They are presented in groups with explanations for size changes.

Group A

Birds in Flight and Pinwheel #3 are continuous designs, with no two dark edges touching and no two light edges touching. For this reason they can be made effectively using only one repeating block. They are equally delightful for use in completely random scrap assortments. The size can be increased as much as you wish, one row at a time, without altering the design.

Group B

Straight Furrows can be enlarged by adding as many rows as you like in either direction. It will certainly be more effective if both block #1 and block #2 are used to separate the lines where dark meets dark and light meets light.

Group C

Streak o' Lightning, Wild Goose Chase, and Wild Geese Flying have one thing in common: any number of rows may be added in length, but two should be added in width to keep the design symmetrical.

Group D

Many Log Cabin patterns have a definite center and so must be increased in size evenly on all four edges. These include Barn Raising, W's, X's, Pinwheels #1 and #2, Starburst, and Sparkling Diamond. In most cases the larger these designs get, the more interesting they become.

Group E

To increase the size of Sea Storm, two rows should be added to both length and width. If they are added along the same edge, the appearance will not change. They may be added one row to an edge for a slightly different effect.

Group F

Sea Horses and Open Windows have bold sixteen-block motifs. To keep this arrangement undisturbed, it is necessary to add four rows to either the length or the width, and always along one edge. New effects may be achieved by treating these designs as though they have definite centers and adding one or two rows to each side and end.

Group G

Joshua's Star and Thistle are best left undisturbed because the centered motif is so important to their appearance. If you want to add to the size in any way except by the addition of borders, you should work out a new diagram on graph paper to see what the effect will be.

Birds in Flight

Pinwheel #3

Straight Furrows

Streak o' Lightning

Wild Goose Chase

Wild Geese Flying

Barn Raising

W's

X's

Pinwheel #1

Pinwheel #2

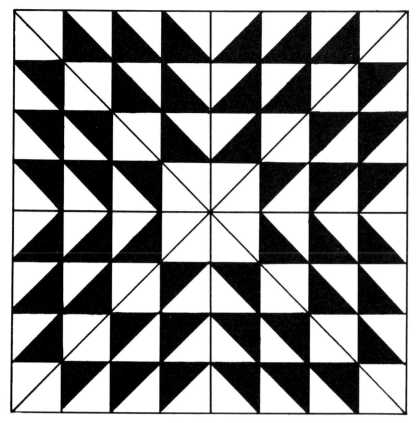

Starburst

Sparkling Diamond

Sea Storm

Sea Horses

Open Windows

Joshua's Star

Thistle

SQUARE BARN RAISING

Square Barn Raising is made by setting the Light and Dark blocks in diagonal rows to form a dark center with alternating light and dark squares around, ending with a dark square. The 8-inch block measures slightly over 11 inches on the diagonal, so the diagram shown is for a piece about 56 inches square. To increase the size the half-row shown will be a row of complete blocks; there will be another complete row and a new row of half-blocks. About 22½ inches will have been added to both length and width, so the new total size will be about 78½ inches square. Because this design forms its own border so nicely, it is customary to finish it with a binding and no extra border—always creating a square quilt.

The triangles for the edge, marked #3 and #4, are made up as square blocks of all dark fabric. Cut A from the same fabric as in the #1 and #2 blocks. Cut B, C, F, G, J, and K of the darks from block #1. Cut D, E, H, I, L, and M of the darks from block #2. When the blocks are cut into triangles, the darks from block #1 will be the #3 pieces and the darks from block #2 will be the #4 pieces. For a quilt in the size shown you will need fifty-six each of blocks #1 and #2 and sixteen of the all-dark blocks to be cut into triangles #3 and #4.

Following piecing Diagram A, join the triangles and blocks in rows. When all the rows have been assembled, lay them out to check accuracy and join the strips to create the effect shown in Diagram B.

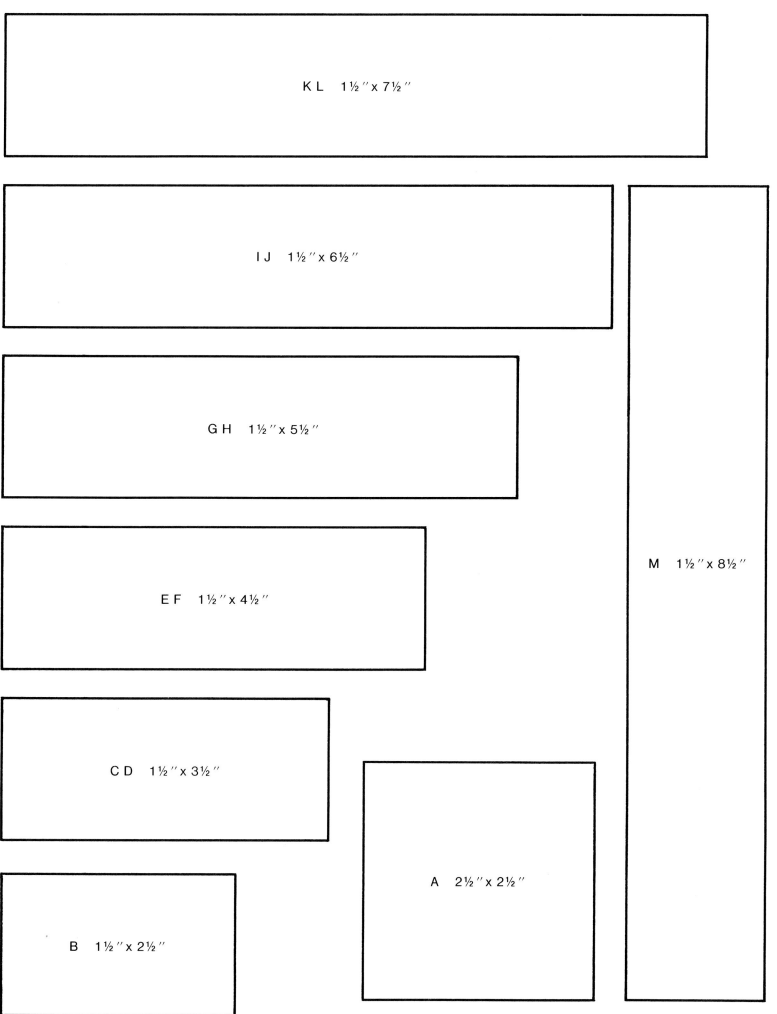

K L   1½″ x 7½″

I J   1½″ x 6½″

G H   1½″ x 5½″

M   1½″ x 8½″

E F   1½″ x 4½″

C D   1½″ x 3½″

A   2½″ x 2½″

B   1½″ x 2½″

Patterns for the Square Barn Raising design. *Note carefully that the ¼-inch seam allowance has already been included in these patterns.*

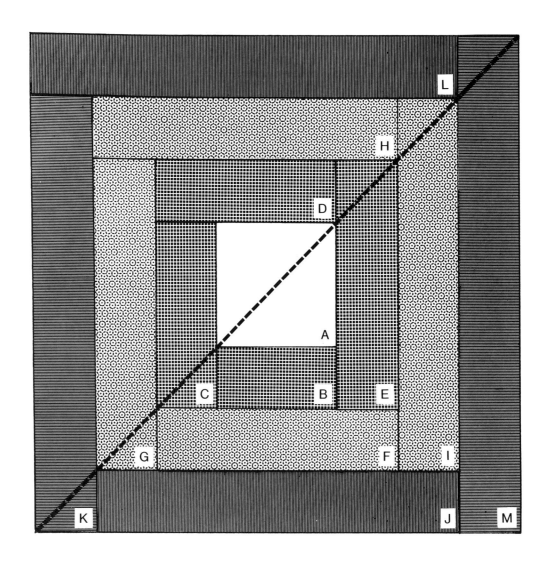

Square Barn Raising edge block #3
Made from the dark fabrics of
Light and Dark block #1
Dotted line for cutting

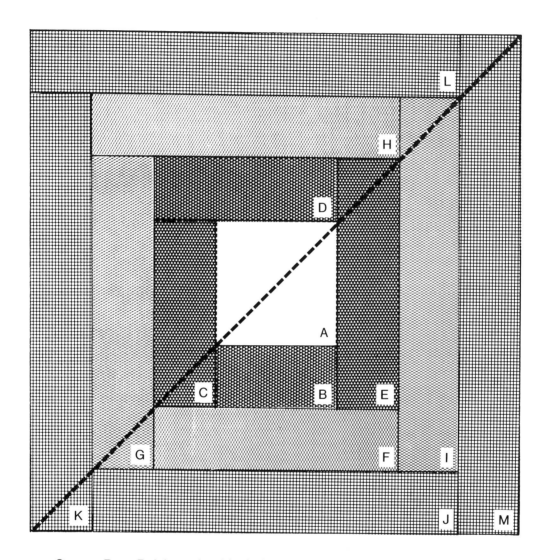

Square Barn Raising edge block #4
Made from the dark fabrics of
Light and Dark block #2
Dotted line for cutting

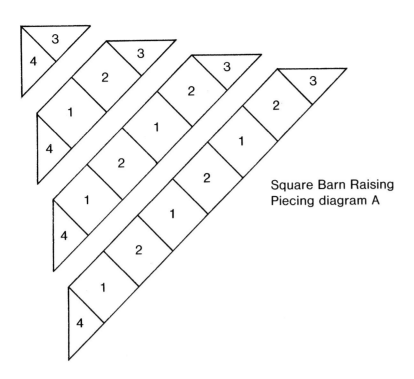

Square Barn Raising
Piecing diagram A

Square Barn Raising
Piecing diagram B

Square Barn Raising shaded diagram

CHEVRON

Another exciting block arrangement can be made from the same pattern pieces used in Light and Dark by setting the strips or "logs" against the square in an asymmetrical design, or Chevron. Seven fabrics are needed: a solid color for the square and six prints or solids for the "logs." Two pieces are cut from each fabric in the following order: B–C, D–E, F–G, H–I, J–K, L–M. The piecing is done as shown in the four order-of-assembly steps.

The blocks can be set square to the edges or diagonal, as shown in the two diagrams. It is not necessary to make blocks from two groups of fabric because the long edge "logs" do not lie against each other as in the Light and Dark arrangements. In the diagonal design, however, a light group and a dark group will make a more exciting contrast.

The edges of the diagonal arrangement make it necessary to cut several blocks in half, either lengthwise or crosswise, and one block into four pieces for the corners. The quilt, as shown, is approximately 56 by 67 inches. Five blocks are cut in two lengthwise for the sides and four crosswise for the ends.

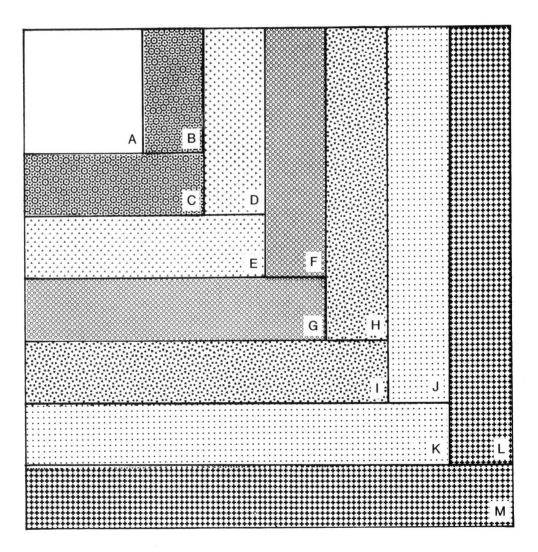

Diagram of complete Chevron block. Use the Light and Dark patterns. Cut A from a solid color. Use six assorted fabrics to cut the twelve "logs," in the following order:
B–C, D–E, F–G, H–I, J–K, and L–M.

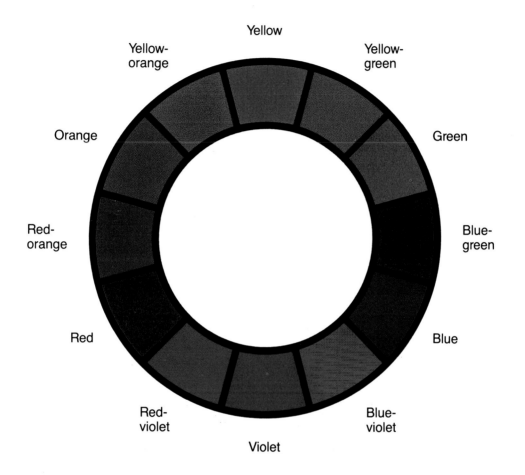

1. Color Wheel

The quilts illustrated in the following color plates are intended to inspire your own Log Cabin projects. Study them closely and savor the many varieties of color and pattern used so expertly in them.

2. Artist unknown: Light and Dark design. c. 1860. Photograph courtesy Phyllis Haders, New York.

3. Carol Anne Wien: Open Windows design. 1977. Quilted by Juanita Whitley. Photograph courtesy the artist.

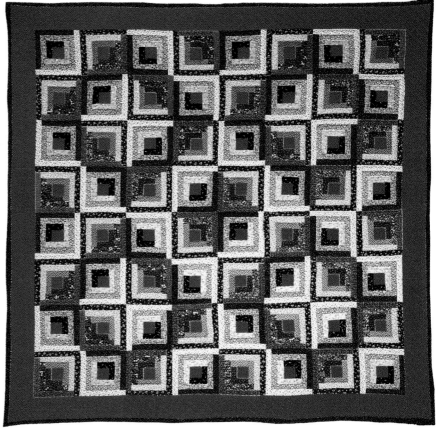

4. Artist unknown: Square Barn Raising design. c. 1880. Photograph courtesy Thos. K. Woodard: American Antiques & Quilts, New York.

5. Carol Anne Wien: Square Barn Raising design. 1977. Quilted by Karen Searle. Photograph courtesy the artist.

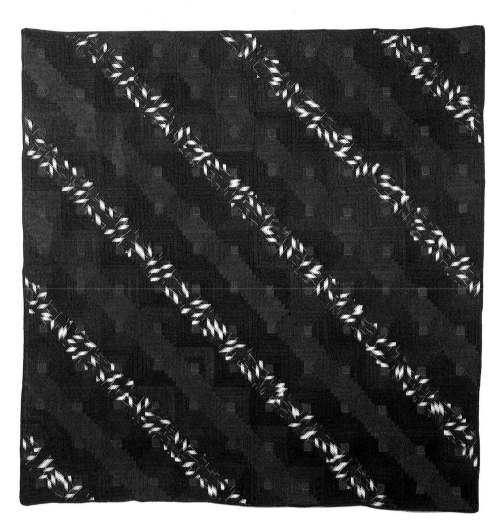

6. Artist unknown: Straight Furrows design. c. 1925. Photograph courtesy America Hurrah Antiques, N.Y.C.

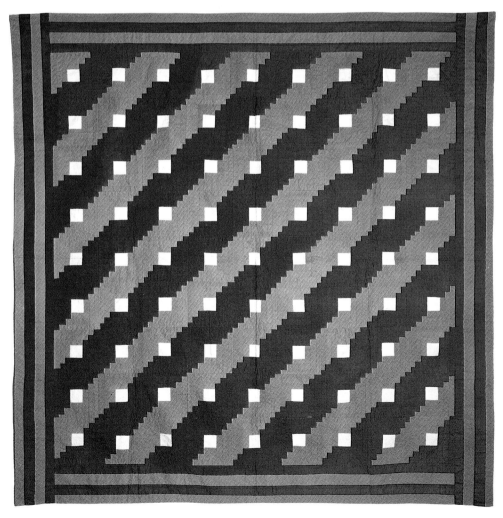

7. Artist unknown: Straight Furrows design. 1890–1910. Photograph courtesy Kiracofe and Kile, San Francisco.

8. Artist unknown: Barn Raising design. c. 1890. Photograph courtesy Bill Gallick and Tony Ellis, New York.

9. Artist unknown: Barn Raising design. c. 1910. Photograph courtesy Kelter-Malcé Antiques, New York.

10. Artist unknown: Barn Raising design. 1900–1910. Photograph courtesy Kelter-Malcé Antiques, New York.

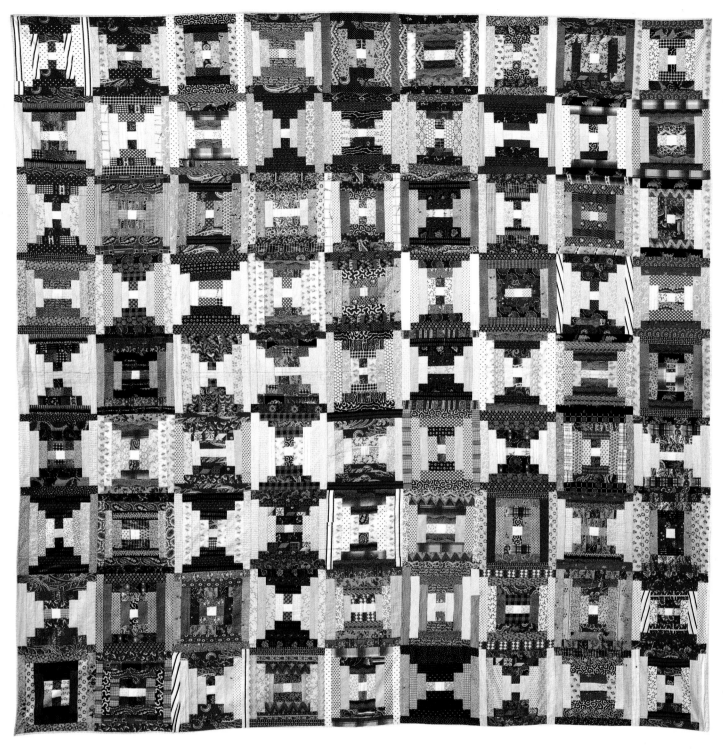

11. Artist unknown: Courthouse Steps design. 1870–1880. Photograph courtesy America Hurrah Antiques, N.Y.C.

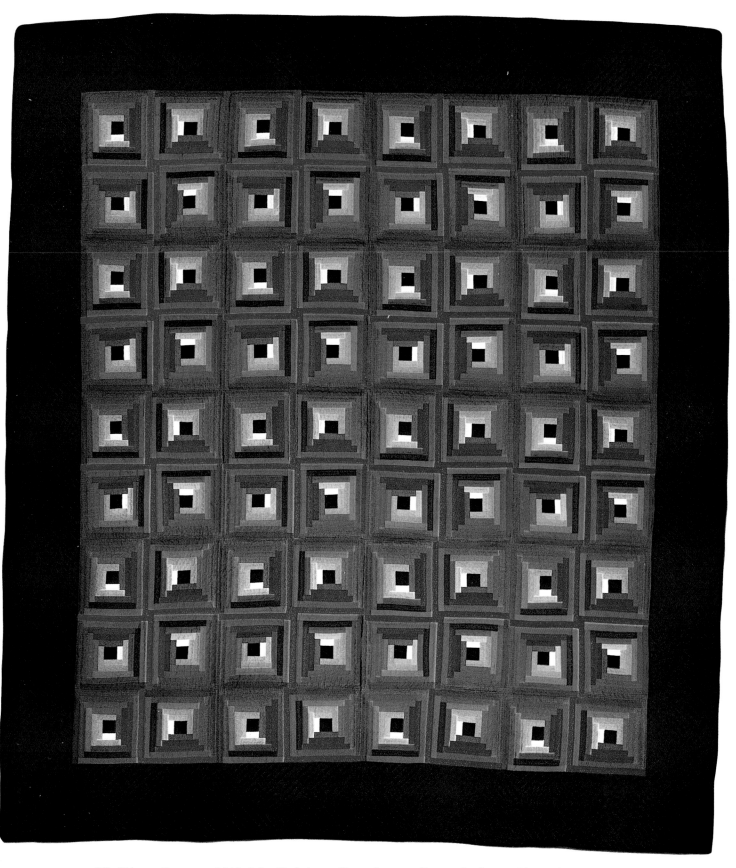

12. Diana Leone: *Midnight Rainbow.* Courthouse Steps design. 1975. Photograph courtesy the artist.

13. Artist unknown: Courthouse Steps design. c. 1885. Photograph courtesy Thos. K. Woodard: American Antiques & Quilts, New York.

14. Carol Anne Wien: Touching Stars design. 1977. Quilted by Barbara Bracanovich. Photograph courtesy the artist.

15. Carol Anne Wien: Chevron design. 1977. Quilted by Barbara Bracanovich. Photograph courtesy the artist.

16. Artist unknown: Streak o' Lightning design. c. 1865. Photograph courtesy America Hurrah Antiques, N.Y.C.

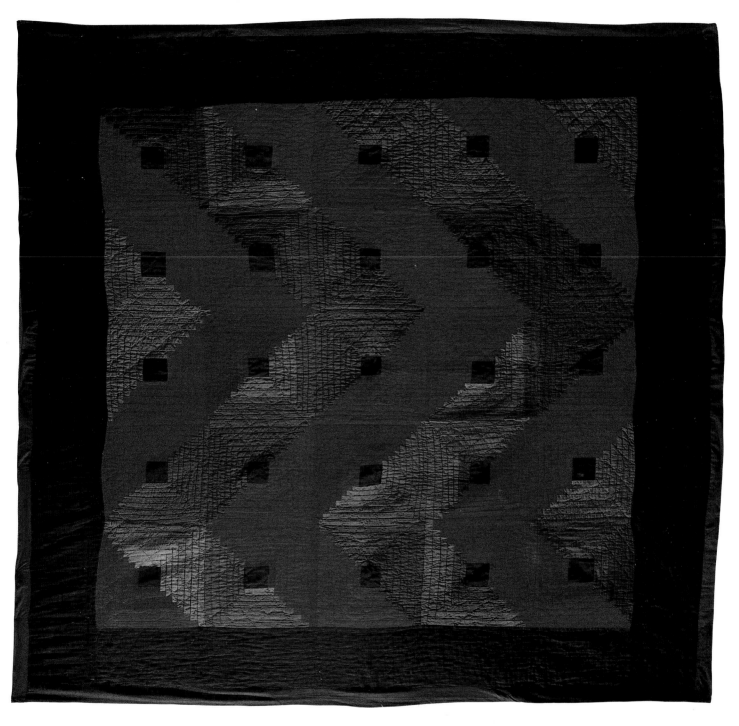

17. Artist unknown: Streak o' Lightning design. c. 1910. Photograph courtesy Kelter-Malcé Antiques, New York.

18. Artist unknown: Original design with Crazy quilt border. c. 1880. Photograph
courtesy Thos. K. Woodard: American Antiques & Quilts, New York.

19. Artist unknown: Streak o' Lightning design variation with Nine Patch centers. c. 1885. Photograph courtesy America Hurrah Antiques, N.Y.C.

20. Artist unknown: Barn Raising design variation with Light and Dark border. c. 1900. Photograph courtesy America Hurrah Antiques, N.Y.C.

21. Carol Anne Wien: X's—Barn Raising design variation. 1977. Quilted by Mrs. R. L. Smith. Photograph courtesy the artist.

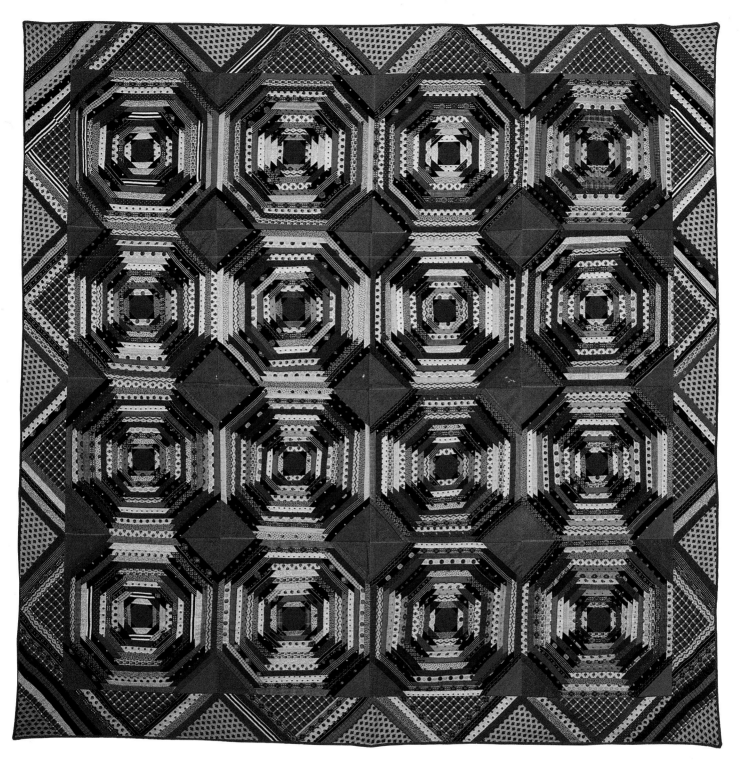

22. Artist unknown: Pineapple design. 1860–1870. Photograph courtesy America Hurrah Antiques, N.Y.C.

23. Leslie C. Carabas: Pineapple design with Wild Goose Chase border. 1980. Quilted by the Five Easy Piecers quilt group. Photograph courtesy the artist.

24. Mary B. Golden: *Ne'er Encounter Pain*. 1982. Pineapple design variation. Photograph by Peter Vandermark courtesy the artist.

25. Diana Leone: *Princess Papulli's Pineapple*. 1983. Photograph courtesy the artist.

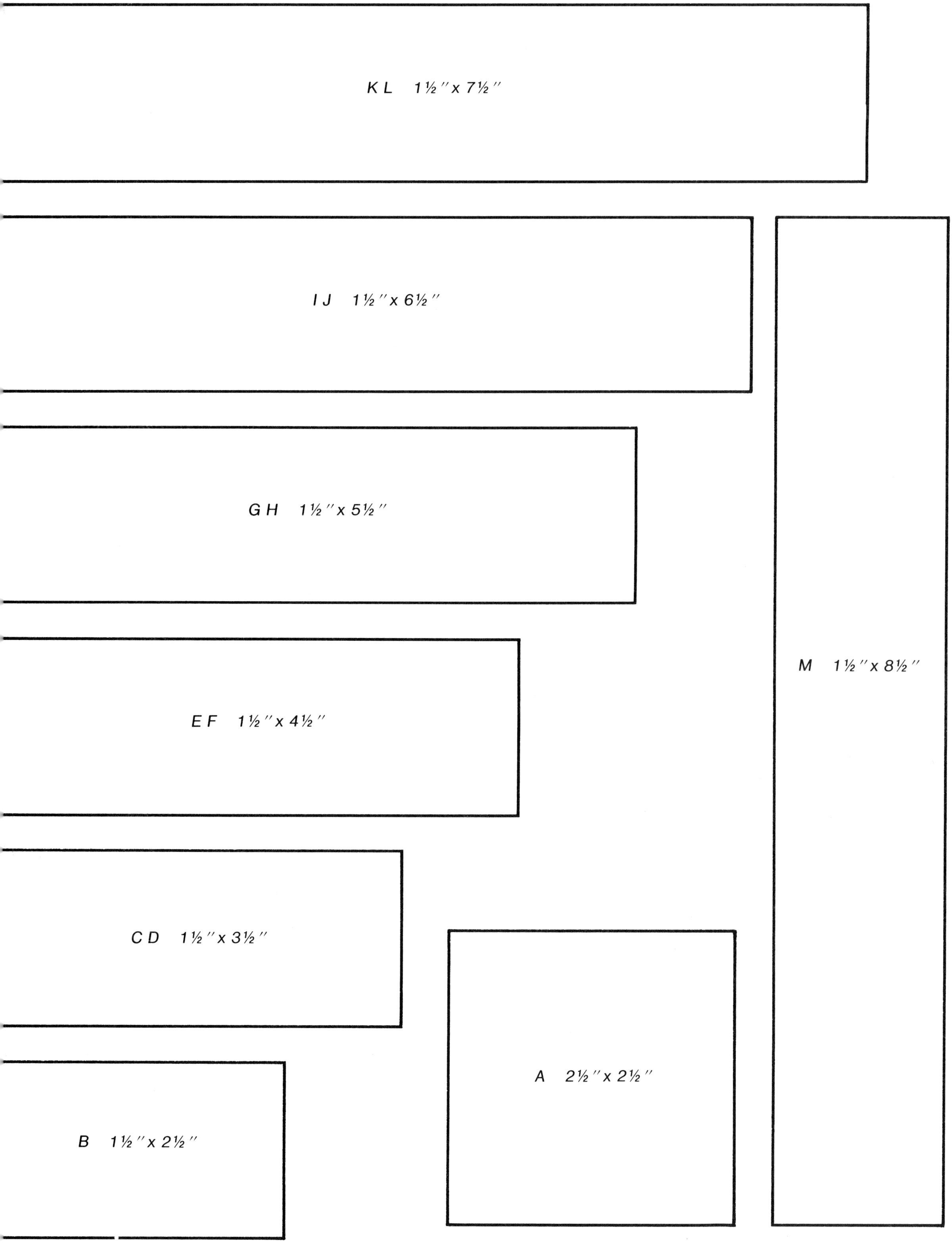

K L   1½" x 7½"

I J   1½" x 6½"

G H   1½" x 5½"

E F   1½" x 4½"

M   1½" x 8½"

C D   1½" x 3½"

A   2½" x 2½"

B   1½" x 2½"

Patterns for the Chevron design. *Note carefully that the ¼-inch seam allowance has already been included in these patterns.*

Chevron order of assembly

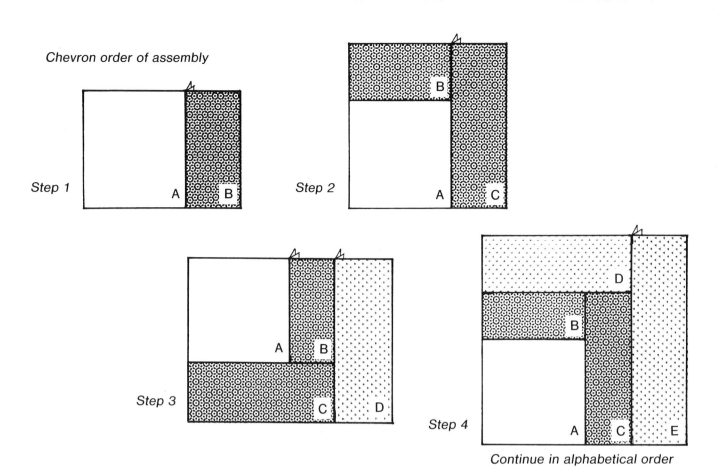

Step 1

Step 2

Step 3

Step 4

Continue in alphabetical order
through step 12

Diagonal Chevron top block #2 and bottom block #2a
Dotted line for cutting

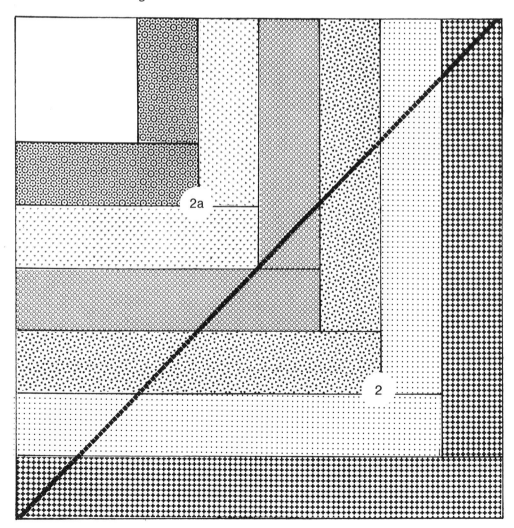

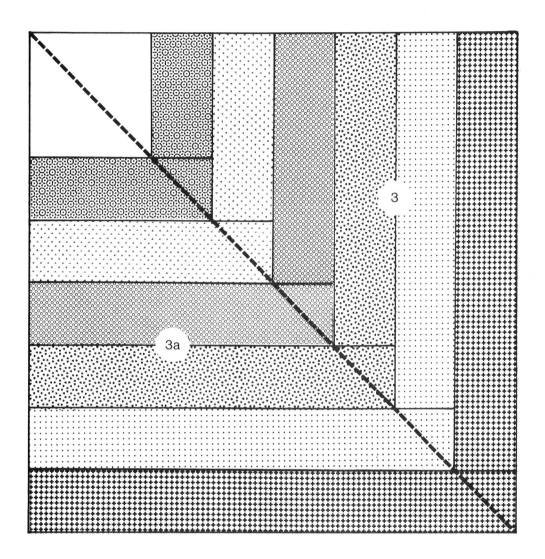

Diagonal Chevron left side block #3
and right side block #3a
Dotted line for cutting

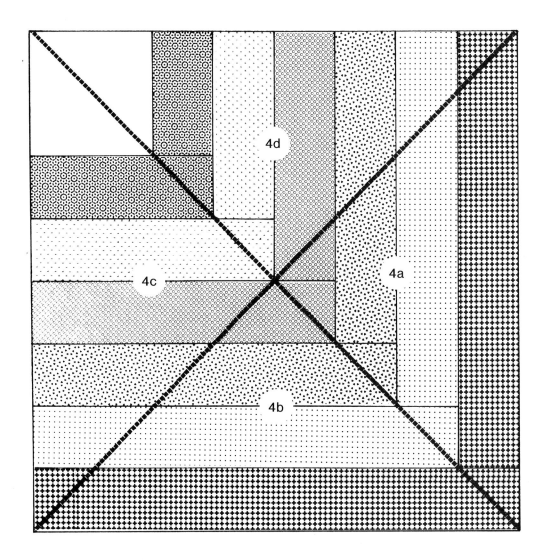

*Diagonal Chevron top left corner
block #4a, top right corner block
#4b, lower right corner block #4c,
and lower left corner block #4d
Dotted line for cutting*

*Chevron shaded diagram showing the square
arrangement of the blocks*

Chevron shaded diagram showing the diagonal arrangement of the blocks

Some More Traditional Patterns

TOUCHING STARS

The same type of block with some new twists and a more complex color arrangement makes the Touching Stars very attractive and somewhat beyond the beginner stage. The first variation is that the 2-inch-square center of each block is made up of three pieces. There are more solid colors used, and it is necessary to set the various blocks together with care to make the contrasts work well.

Each of the 16-block sections makes a large Sawtooth Star design, and the whole piece has a very definite center. It is difficult to enlarge the 64-inch square pattern in any way except with borders without upsetting its balance.

Note that the white areas in the order-of-assembly diagrams represent a solid color, which appears as dark in all the other diagrams. The same solid color is used for all pieces of block #1 and for D–E, H–I, and L–M of blocks #2 and #3. Four prints each are used in blocks #2 and #3, from which B–C, F–G, J–K, and N–O are cut. Make twelve of block #1, forty-two of block #2, and ten of block #3.

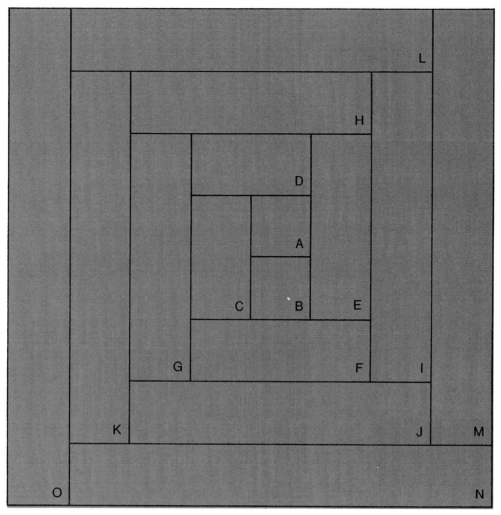

Touching Stars block #1

*Touching Stars
order of assembly
block #1
all solid color*

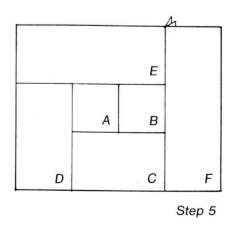

Step 1

Step 2

Step 3

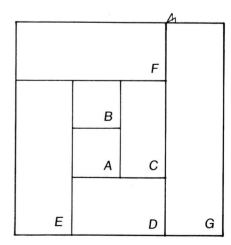

Step 4

Step 5

Continue in alphabetical order through step 14

Step 6

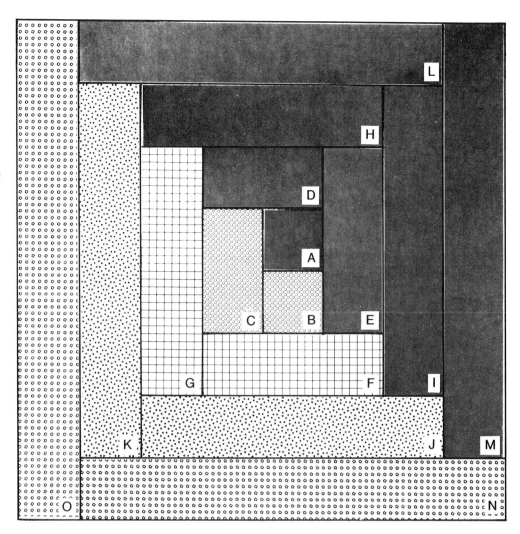

Touching Stars block #2

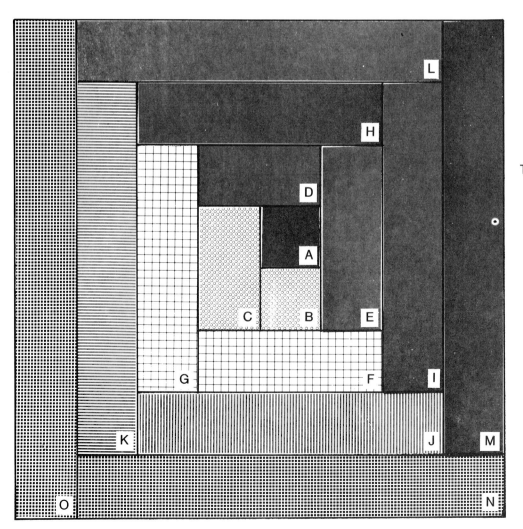

Touching Stars block #3

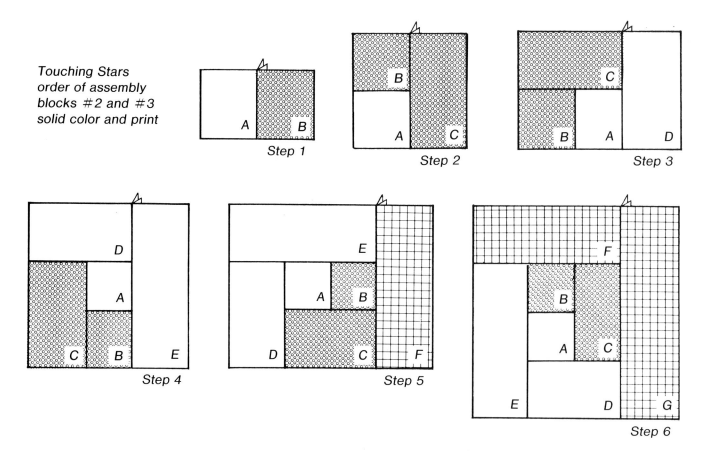

Touching Stars order of assembly blocks #2 and #3 solid color and print

Step 1

Step 2

Step 3

Step 4

Step 5

Step 6

Continue in alphabetical order through step 14

Touching Stars piecing diagram with numbered blocks

1	2	2	1	1	2	2	1
2	3	2	2	2	3	2	2
2	2	3	2	2	2	3	2
1	2	2	3	2	2	2	1
1	2	2	2	3	2	2	1
2	3	2	2	2	3	2	2
2	2	3	2	2	2	3	2
1	2	2	1	1	2	2	1

Patterns for the Touching Stars design. *Note carefully that the ¼-inch seam allowance has already been included in these patterns.*

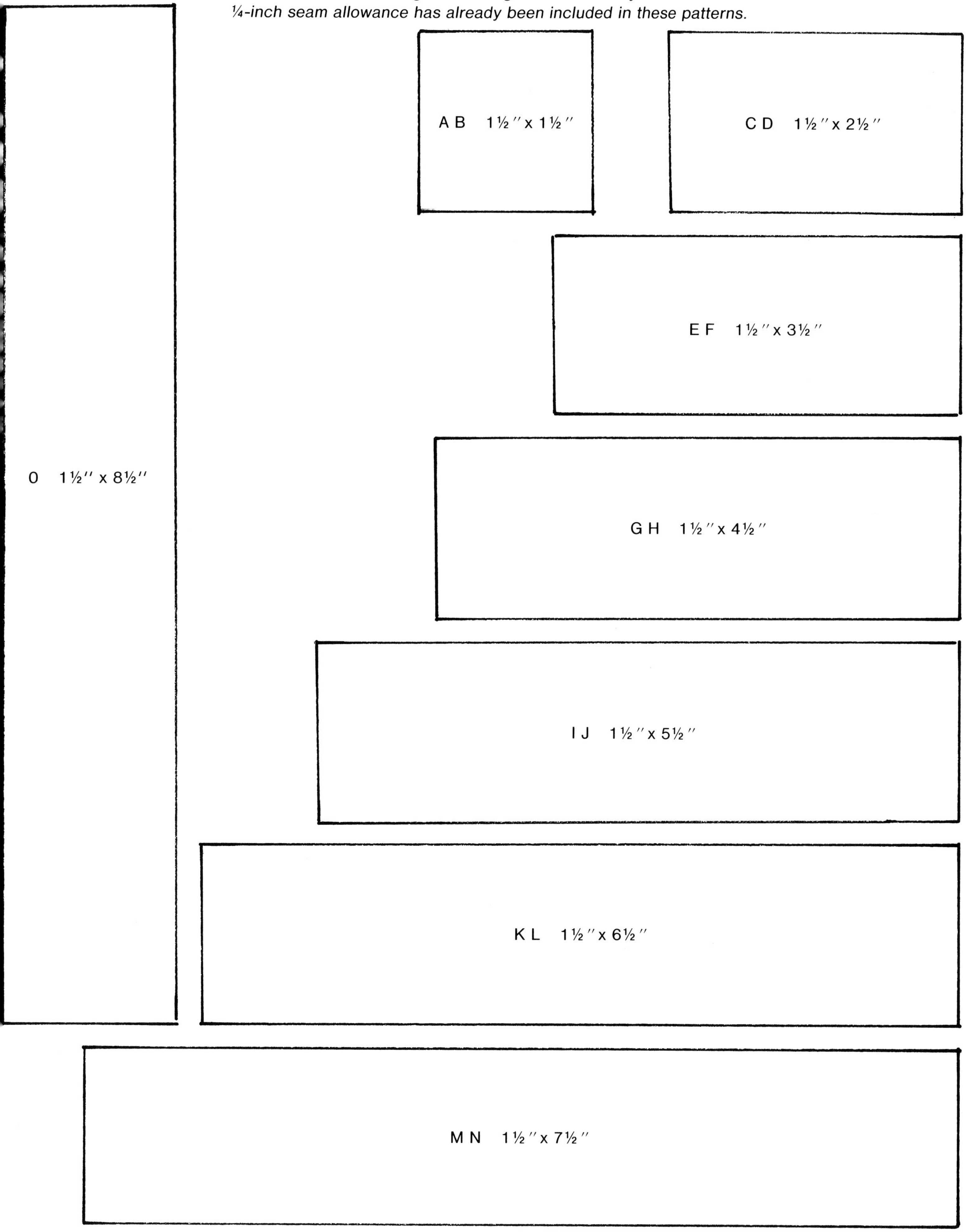

A B   1½″ x 1½″

C D   1½″ x 2½″

E F   1½″ x 3½″

G H   1½″ x 4½″

I J   1½″ x 5½″

K L   1½″ x 6½″

M N   1½″ x 7½″

O   1½″ x 8½″

Touching Stars shaded diagram showing the arrangement of the blocks

COURTHOUSE STEPS

The precise symmetry of the Courthouse Steps block does not lend itself to the many variations of the Light and Dark blocks, but can be given some variation and sparkle. The two-block system, using the same solid color for both centers and eight different prints for the "logs" in each block, lightens the appearance, preventing the double effect where the outside "logs" meet. The direction of the blocks can also be varied so that the centers run alternately vertical and horizontal. Another variation is called White House Steps (page 81).

Use four light and four dark print fabrics for each Courthouse Steps block. Cut two of each "log" from each fabric, B–B, D–D, F–F, and H–H from the light, and C–C, E–E, G–G, and I–I from the dark, as shown in the block #1 and block #2 diagrams.

When the blocks are set together, they form no secondary pattern, so the size of the quilt may be increased by any number of rows in either direction. The block size is 10 inches square, so the plan shown is for a 50-by-70-inch quilt.

One word of warning: the blocks are so symmetrical and the lines of the design so square that very even piecing is necessary. No diagonal line forms as a secondary pattern to distract the eye from uneven blocks and lines that wobble, so the best effect is gained from absolute perfection.

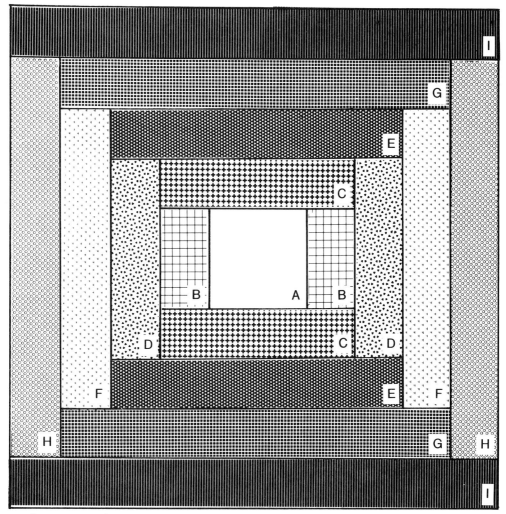

Courthouse Steps block #1

Courthouse Steps order of assembly

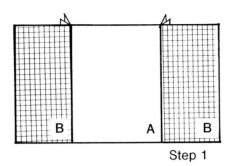

Step 1

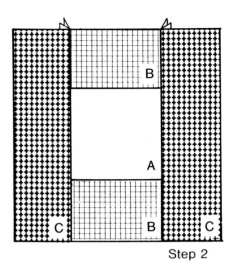

Step 2

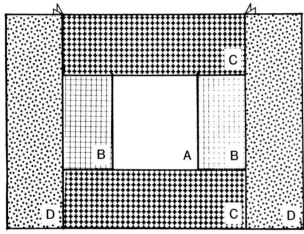

Step 3

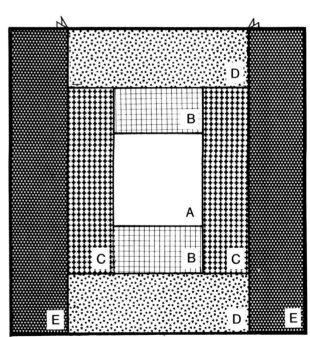

Step 4

Continue in alphabetical order through step 8

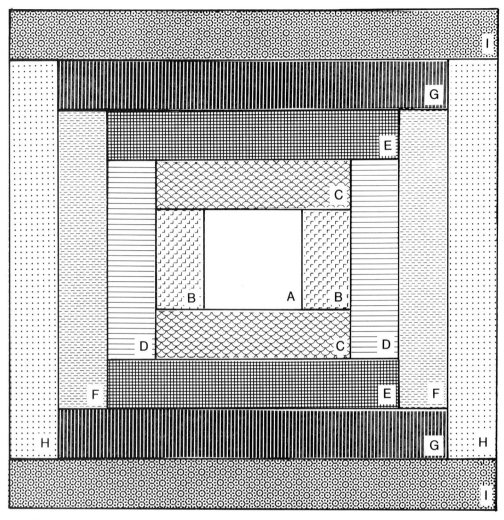

Courthouse Steps block #2

Patterns for the Courthouse Steps design. *Note carefully that the ¼-inch seam allowance has already been included in these patterns.*

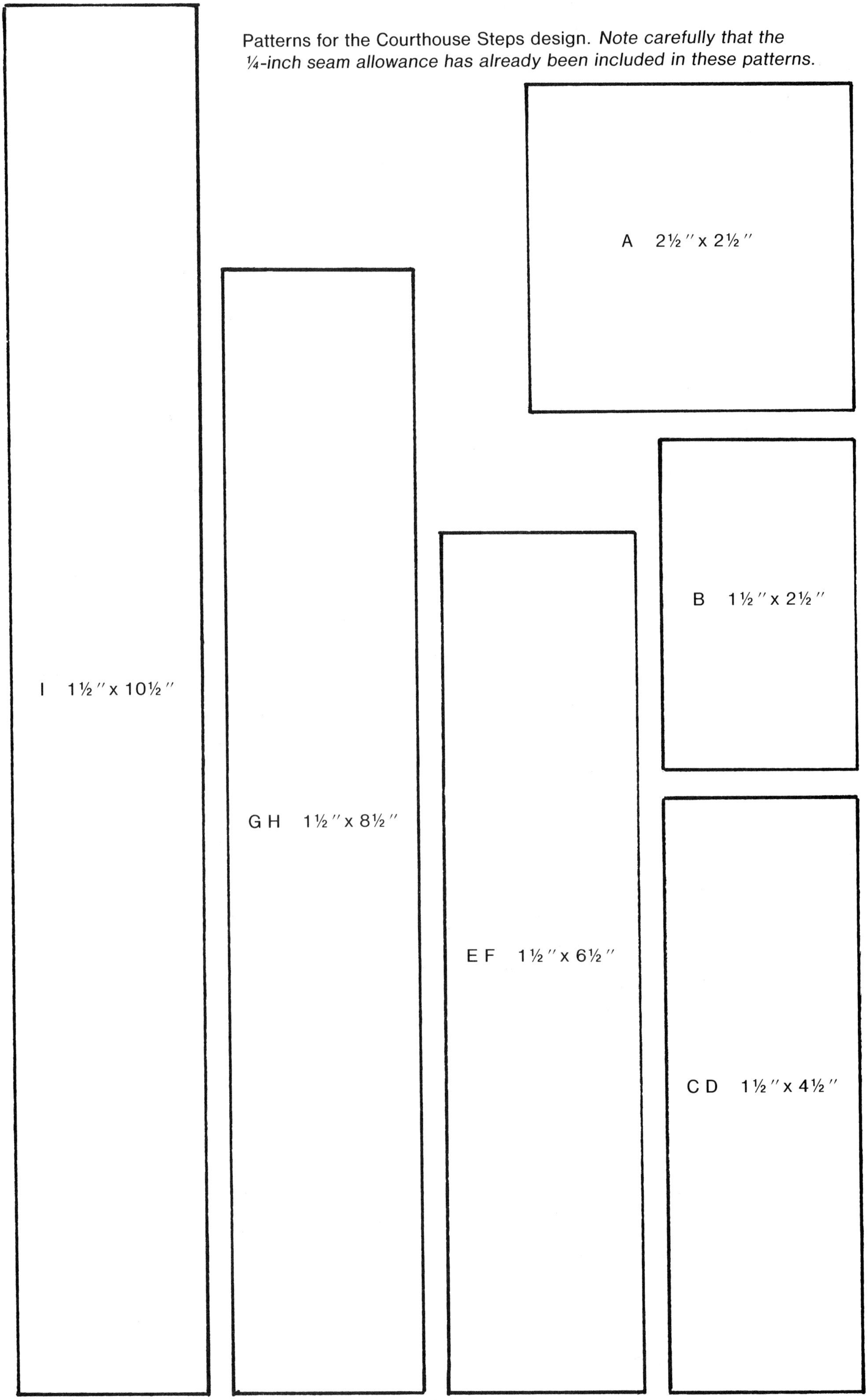

A   2½″ x 2½″

I   1½″ x 10½″

G H   1½″ x 8½″

B   1½″ x 2½″

E F   1½″ x 6½″

C D   1½″ x 4½″

Courthouse Steps shaded diagram showing a basic arrangement
of the blocks

Courthouse Steps shaded diagram showing an arrangement with
alternate blocks turned

WHITE HOUSE STEPS

Another very precise square design is created with the same patterns as used for Courthouse Steps—and only four colors or prints, two light and two dark, besides the center piece, in each block. The fabrics are alternated in rows around the center, B–B and C–C from one print, D–D and E–E from another, F–F and G–G from a third, and H–H and I–I from the fourth. In the diagram shown half the blocks have the light fabric on the outside (H–H and I–I) row, and half have the dark on that row. For further variation and sparkle the two-block system can be used. Neat and even piecing with all the lines very straight will do more for the final appearance of this very square design than efforts at originality.

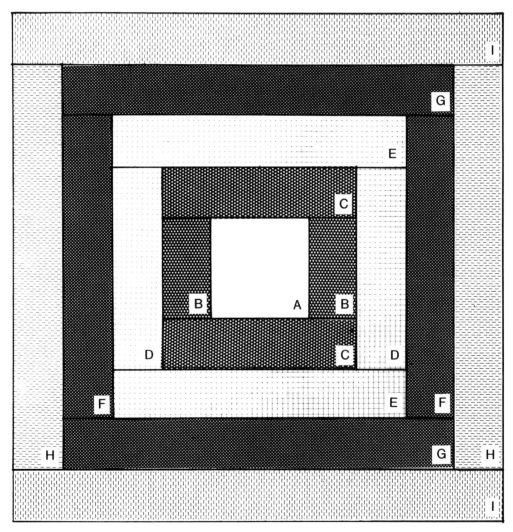

White House Steps block #1

White House Steps order of assembly

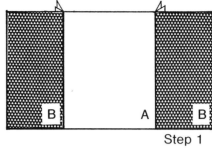

Step 1

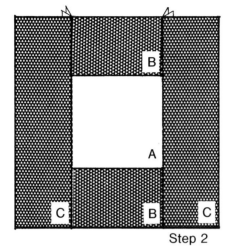

Step 2

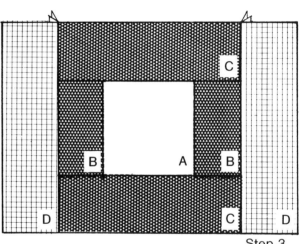

Step 3

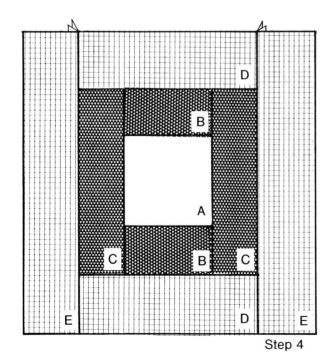

Step 4

Continue in alphabetical order through step 8

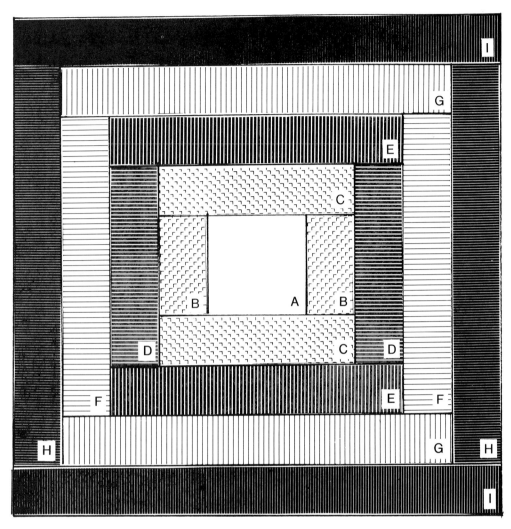

White House Steps block #2

Patterns for the White House Steps design. *Note carefully that the ¼-inch seam allowance has already been included in these patterns.*

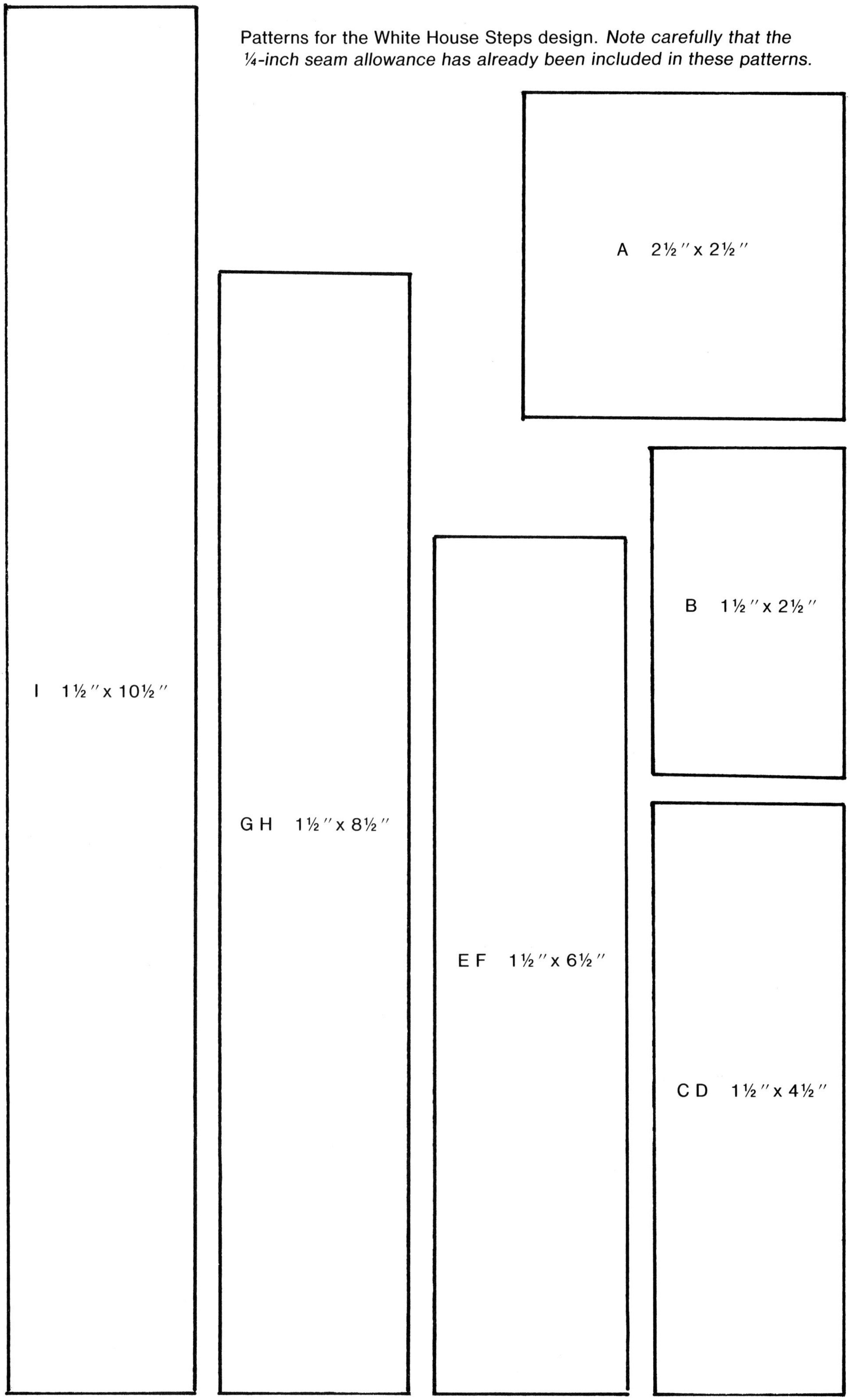

A   2½″ x 2½″

B   1½″ x 2½″

I   1½″ x 10½″

G H   1½″ x 8½″

E F   1½″ x 6½″

C D   1½″ x 4½″

White House Steps shaded diagram showing the arrangement
of the blocks

PINEAPPLE

Of all the traditional Log Cabin designs, the Pineapple certainly holds top place for complexity, motion, and excitement. It is also the most difficult to plan and assemble. Though there are only nine pattern pieces, there are fifteen strip designations or placements. Except in the case of the center—A—piece, each piece must be cut four times in each designated fabric, four light B, four dark C, and so forth.

It is not necessary to use two blocks of totally different fabrics, but the last—L—"log" may be made of one fabric in half the blocks and another fabric in the other half so that the double "log" at meeting sides is avoided. In planning fabrics and yardage, you will need, as in any Log Cabin block, a solid color for the center square. Then you will need eight darks and seven lights (allowing for the two different lights used for L).

Many antique Pineapples were constructed from scrap or random fabrics, as were so many other Log Cabins, but the placement of light and dark was all-important. It is possible to use a basic fifteen prints, as mentioned above, and to mix or jumble them, or add a few scrap pieces for spice. Cutting and planning will become more difficult but often rewarding in this free-style design.

Cutting and Assembling the Pineapple

The same methods of cutting 1½-inch strips that are used for all the other Log Cabin blocks may be used for the Pineapple (see Chapter II). Cardboard templates for B and C "logs" must be made with the corners cut off. On all the other templates you have two choices: with corner-cut templates (Method I) or with rectangular templates (Method II). In the latter method the corners will be cut after the rectangles are joined to the center piece. In either method of piecing it is necessary to see that seam widths and "log" widths remain absolutely constant and that stitching lines are perfectly straight. Because of the more complicated shape and larger format of the Pineapple block, small mistakes tend to multiply as you go outward and therefore to become more obvious than in the simpler four-sided Log Cabin designs.

The first four steps for both methods are identical, as shown in the diagrams. In Method I all the corners are cut off ahead of seaming, and the piecing continues as shown in Steps 5 and 6. In Method II the rectangular strips are attached and then cut, as shown in Steps 5 and 6. You may do this on the paper cutter or by hand. When you make test blocks, you can experiment to see which method works best for you. Only the final results matter.

Quilting the Pineapple is not too different from quilting any other Log Cabin design, except that, after going around the little A piece, you will be working around an eight-sided figure, a slightly uneven octagon. On L, M, and N you will stop at the ends, not completing the octagon. On O the quilting will be carried all the way around the triangle, as shown in the diagram. By treating these last strips in a different manner from the central octagon shape, you will be subtly accentuating the square areas that act as a joining for the octagons. In some old Pineapple quilts the M–N–O area was treated as one triangle, often in black, thus completely dividing the octagons and making the pineapple shape more apparent.

Diagram of complete Pineapple block.

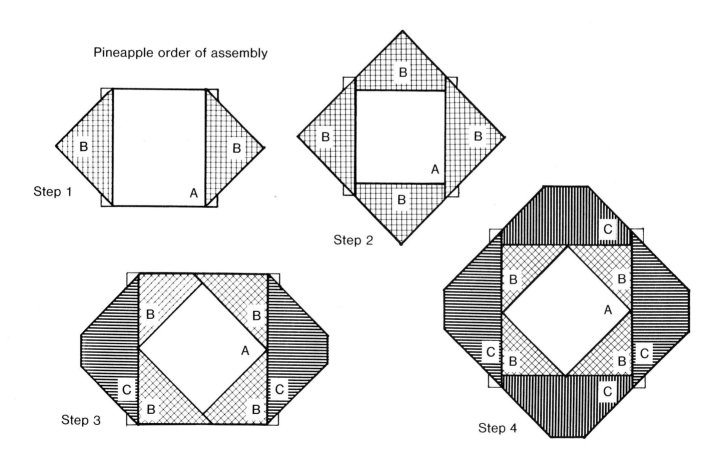

Pineapple order of assembly

Step 1

Step 2

Step 3

Step 4

Method I Pineapple assembly showing log D with the angles cut before they are joined to the preceding row C.

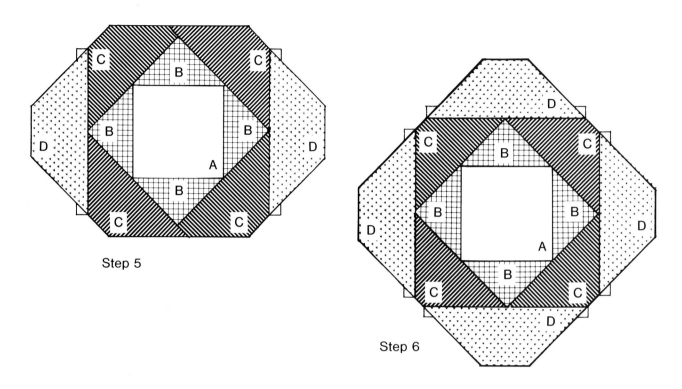

Step 5

Step 6

Method II Pineapple assembly showing log D in its rectangular form joined to the preceding row C. Angles are cut after stitching, using the outer edge of row C as the guide line.

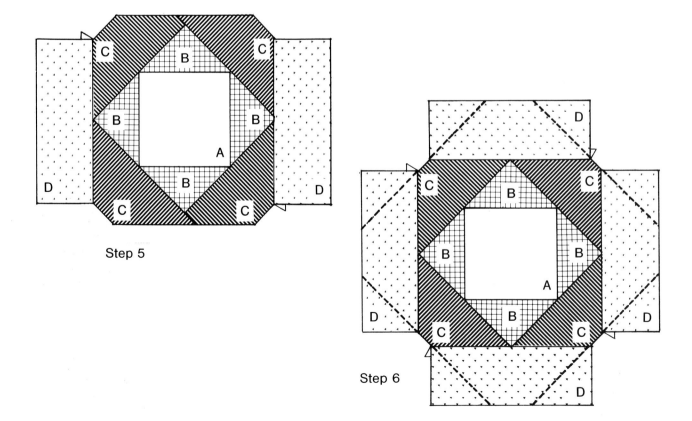

Step 5

Step 6

Patterns for the Pineapple design. *Note carefully that the ¼-inch seam allowance has already been included in these patterns.*

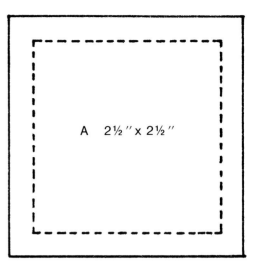

A   2½ " x 2½ "

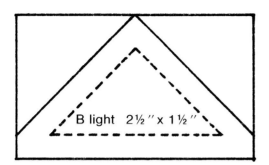

B light 2½ " x 1½ "

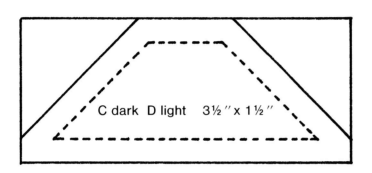

C dark D light   3½ " x 1½ "

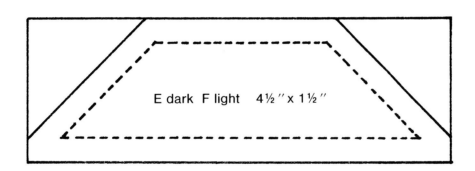

E dark F light   4½ " x 1½ "

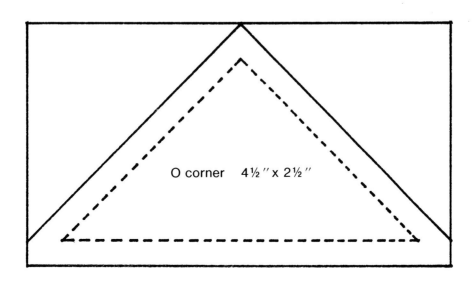

O corner   4½ " x 2½ "

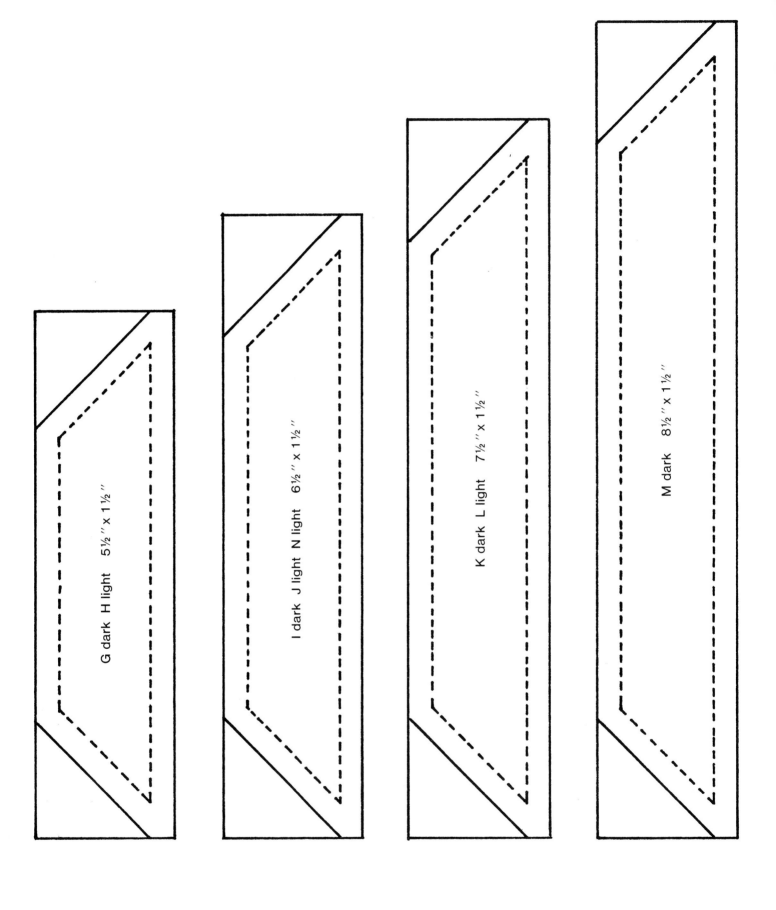

G dark H light   5½″ x 1½″

I dark J light N light   6½″ x 1½″

K dark L light   7½″ x 1½″

M dark   8½″ x 1½″

Quilting the Pineapple block

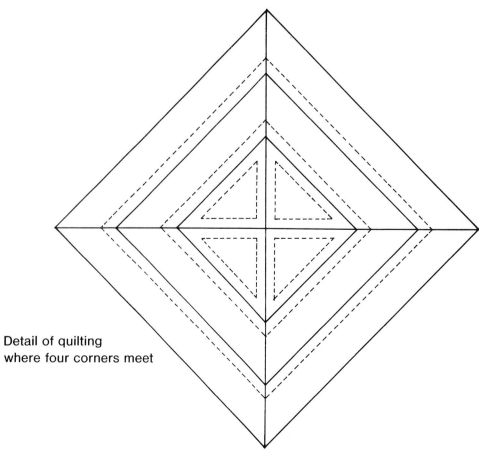

Detail of quilting
where four corners meet

The effect of the quilting on four blocks joined

Pineapple shaded diagram

The Log Cabin Dances to a New Tune

No sooner does a quilter invent a pattern than other quilters start inventing variations, new dimensions, new ways of color planning, and original versions bearing almost no resemblance to the first. No one knows who put together the first Log Cabin, but the last word has certainly not been said. A charming design first made of the "strings" of fabric left over in an age when frugal cutting was a necessity soon grew into an artist's challenge.

In the late 19th century, when silk and velvet "throws" were more popular than full bed quilts, the Log Cabin shone in bejeweled splendor. Tiny strips of the finest dress fabrics and ribbons were put together in infinite numbers of rows to create elaborate Courthouse Steps and Pineapple designs.

The late 20th century has again brought the versatile Log Cabin out of obscurity. It blooms in fresh new prints, brave contemporary shapes, and arrangements that make it rank high in quilters' popularity polls. Few quilters can pass up the chance to change and improve upon this charming and versatile design, once they've made one of the basic styles already described.

You may still want to work from the traditional Straight Furrows, Barn Raising, or Courthouse Steps, varying the fabrics and the dimensions. If you are using scrap-bag fabrics, you will first need to separate them into groups of light and dark. There are medium shades, as mentioned in the section on color, that can be used in either the light or dark areas, often both in the same quilt. If the weights of the fabrics vary greatly, you may need to experiment with them to see that they can be used together successfully. A sheer dotted Swiss or a slippery silk crepe often requires a backing of a firm, thin underlining fabric to make it compatible to the heavier cottons or velvets that will make up the rest of the block. A very lightweight iron-on backing, such as Featherweight Pellon, often works well and is easy to handle. Another alternative, especially if all the fabrics are difficult to handle, is the press-piece method (p. 15).

All of the designs shown may be miniaturized, but more skill is needed to sew ½-inch "logs" than 1-inch ones. It is wise to make up paper patterns and to check out a sample block if you want to change sizes. Remember that a seam allowance is always needed; ¼ inch is the most satisfactory. That means that for a ½-inch "log" you must cut a 1-inch strip.

Borders and color arrangements can vary greatly from the ones described in the early chapters. You have only to look at the great variety of spectacular quilts illustrated in the color plates to realize how many exciting things you can do even with the patterns given. An entire color spectrum can be worked into one Pineapple quilt. Borders can be made up of "string" pieces or Victorian Crazy quilting. Although some of the quilts shown in color are made by the author, following the directions exactly, many are highly original pieces, both antique and contemporary, which have been included to provide inspiration for the adventurous quilter.

Another way of venturing into the world of unusual Log Cabins is by taking up the challenge of some fascinating contemporary shapes. Included in this last section are patterns and basic plans for Hexagons, Triangles, Diamonds and Parallelograms, and off-center designs to be used as suggested or in even newer designs of your own invention.

HEXAGON

The arrangement of the Hexagon shown here is made from light, dark, and medium fabrics, either planned or scrap. From light fabric cut two each of B, E, H, K, N, and Q. From medium fabric cut two each of C, F, I, L, O, and R. From dark fabric cut two each of D, G, J, M, P, and S.

Lay the B pieces right sides together with the A center piece, opposite each other as shown in the piecing diagram, then pin the seam lines together and stitch. Press the seams away from the center. Continue to join the pieces on opposite sides in alphabetical order, pressing the seams after each stitching. Some fabrics are more mobile than others, occasionally making it necessary to trim the angles slightly after stitching to keep the next edge absolutely straight.

The hexagons can be joined in rows, as shown in the shaded diagram, so that like color values meet. Joining the rows together is not so easy and you may well want to seam these indented edges by hand. If you are skilled at machine sewing, you will be able to stop the stitching of the first short seams exactly where the marked seamline stops and backstitch, leaving an opening between each hexagon in which to fit the next row of hexagons so that you can machine stitch the sides one at a time between the rows, again backstitching at each seam end.

The blocks on the ends and sides will have to be cut in half, as with the Square Barn Raising, and the other half used at the opposite end or side; see assembly procedure. It is possible to use quarter blocks in the corners or to avoid them, depending upon the number of blocks in each direction and how you want them arranged. A border can be added or not, as you choose.

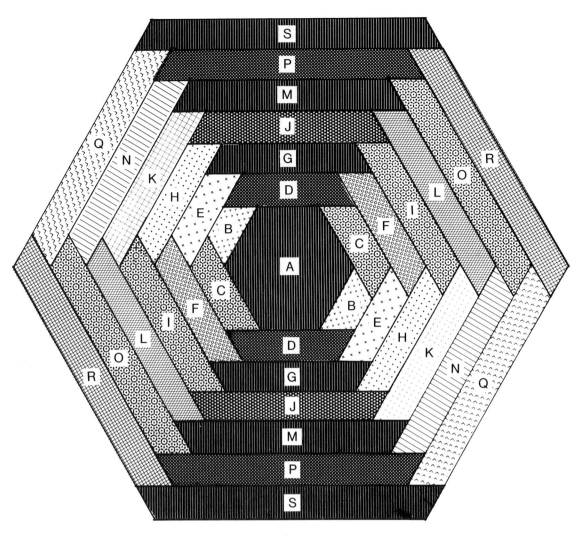

Diagram of complete Hexagon block, using light,
medium, and dark fabrics.

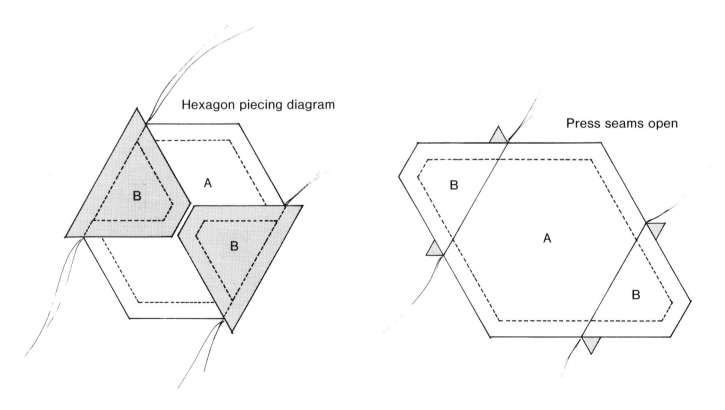

Hexagon piecing diagram

Press seams open

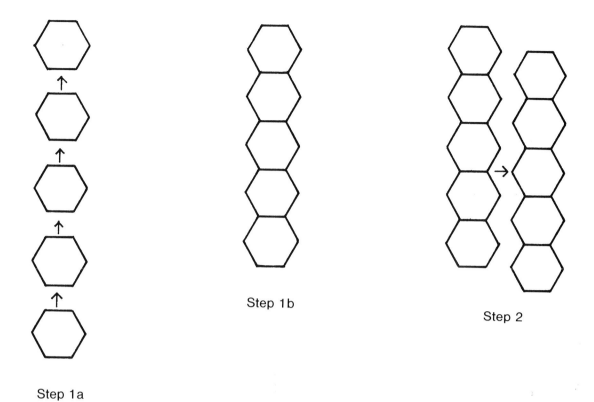

Step 1a

Step 1b

Step 2

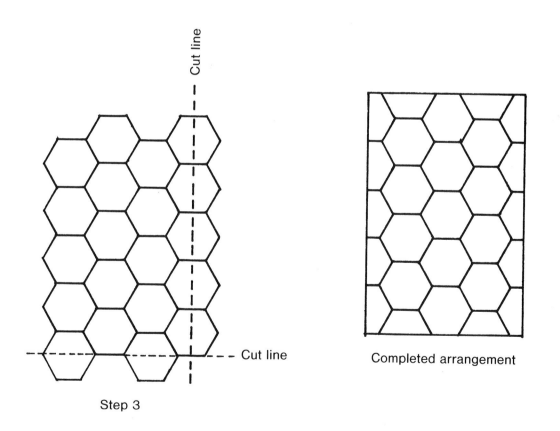

Cut line

Cut line

Step 3

Completed arrangement

Hexagon quilt assembly procedure

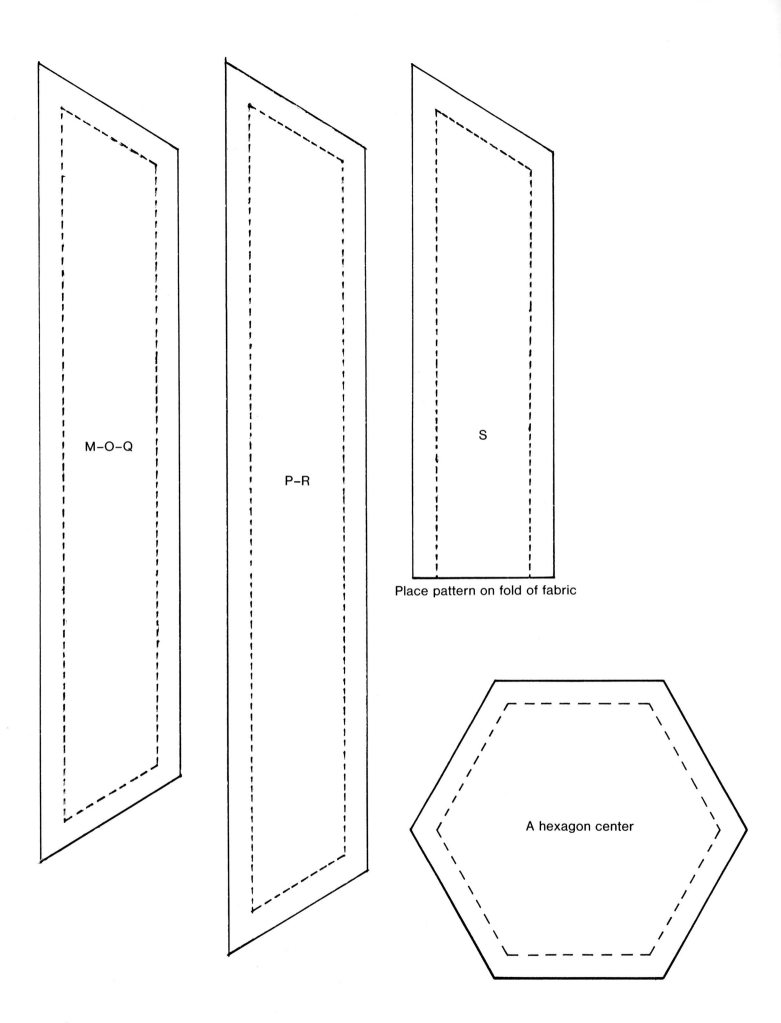

M–O–Q

P–R

S

Place pattern on fold of fabric

A hexagon center

Patterns for the Hexagon design. *Note carefully that the ¼-inch seam allowance has already been included in these patterns.*

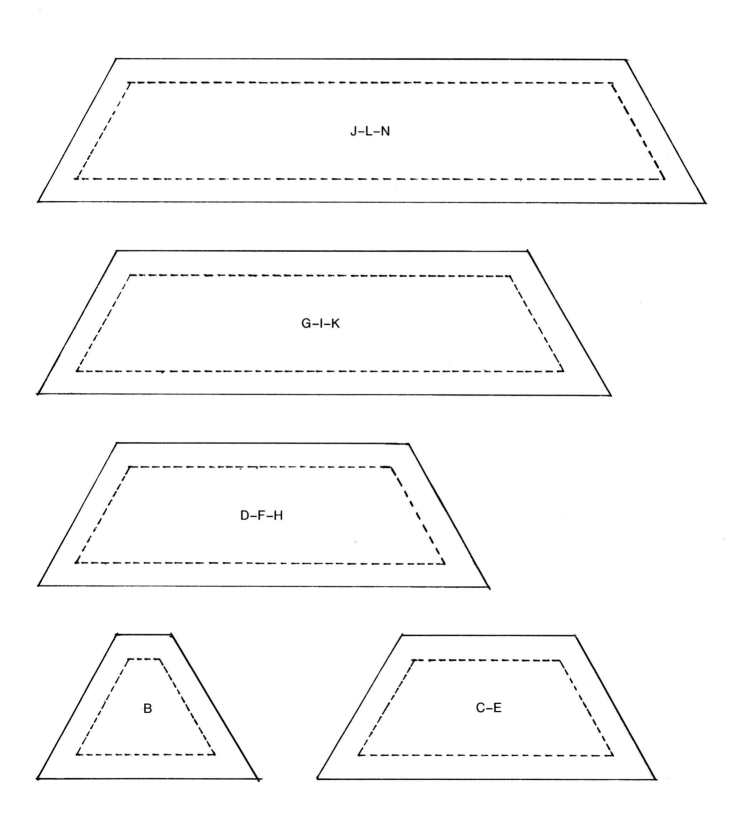

Hexagon arrangement showing blocks cut for sides and corners

Hexagon shaded diagram showing the three-tone
arrangement of the blocks.

TRIANGLE

You will undoubtedly be able to use the triangle Log Cabin pattern in some other interesting arrangement, but the alternating light and dark one shown here is a fine one in terms of its startling contrasts. The dark center in the light block and the light center in the dark make an interesting interplay of color. You may work with as few as six fabrics or as many scrap pieces as you like.

For block #1 cut A in any dark fabric. Cut B, C, and D in one light fabric. Cut E, F, and G in a second light fabric. Cut H, I, and J in the third light fabric. For block #2 cut A in any light fabric. Cut B, C, and D in one dark fabric. Cut E, F, and G in a second dark fabric. Cut H, I, and J in a third dark fabric.

Lay the B piece right sides together with the A center piece, pin the seam lines together, and stitch. Press the seams away from the center. Continue to join the pieces in clockwise progression and alphabetical order, pressing the seams after each stitching.

The blocks can be joined, alternating light and dark to form rows. The rows will be set together in a diagonal arrangement as can be seen in the shaded diagram. The blocks along the sides must be cut in half as in the hexagon. It is wise to sketch a diagram showing the number of blocks you plan to use. You will then see that each row increases in length and will be able to judge exactly how many blocks and rows you need.

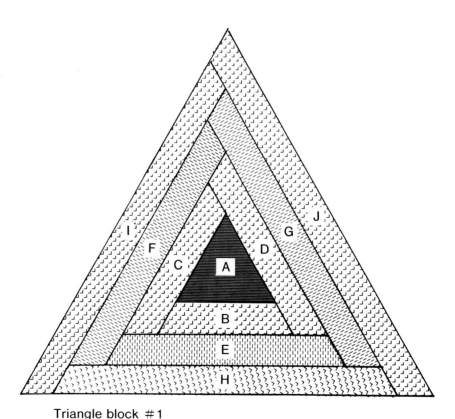

Triangle block #1

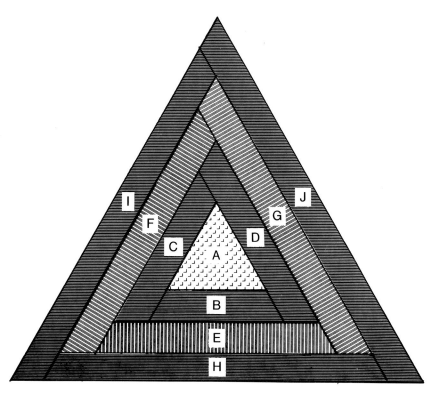

Triangle block #2

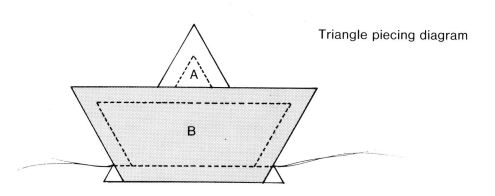

Triangle piecing diagram

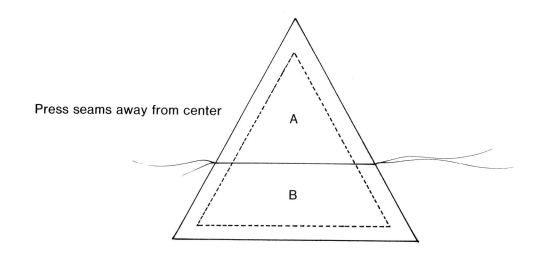

Press seams away from center

103

Triangle quilt assembly procedure

Step 1

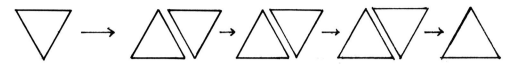

Step 2

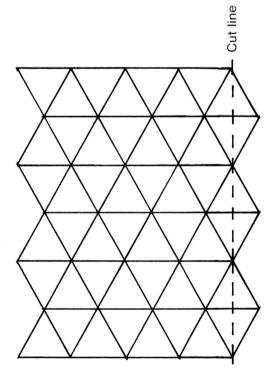

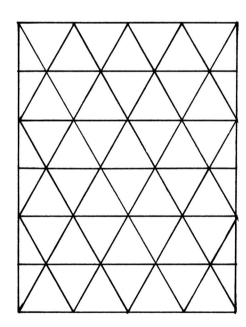

Cut line

Step 3

Completed arrangement

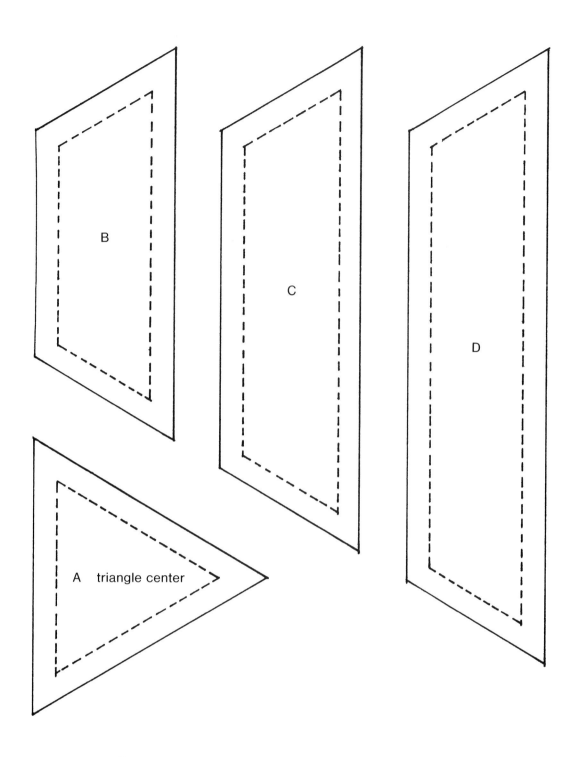

Patterns for Triangle design. *Note carefully that ¼-inch seam allowance has already been included in these patterns.*

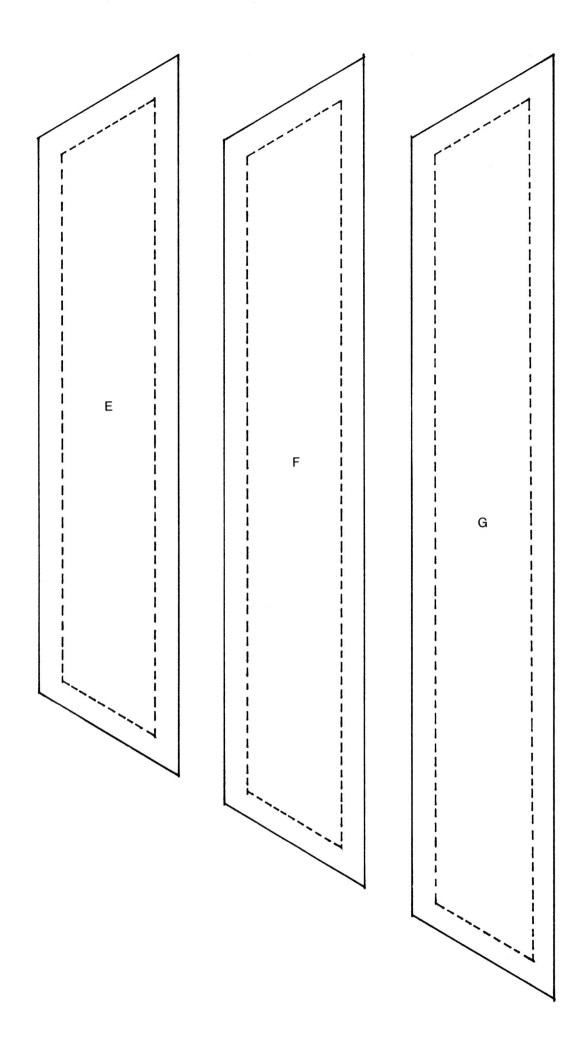

Place pattern
on fold of fabric

Place pattern
on fold of fabric

Place pattern
on fold of fabric

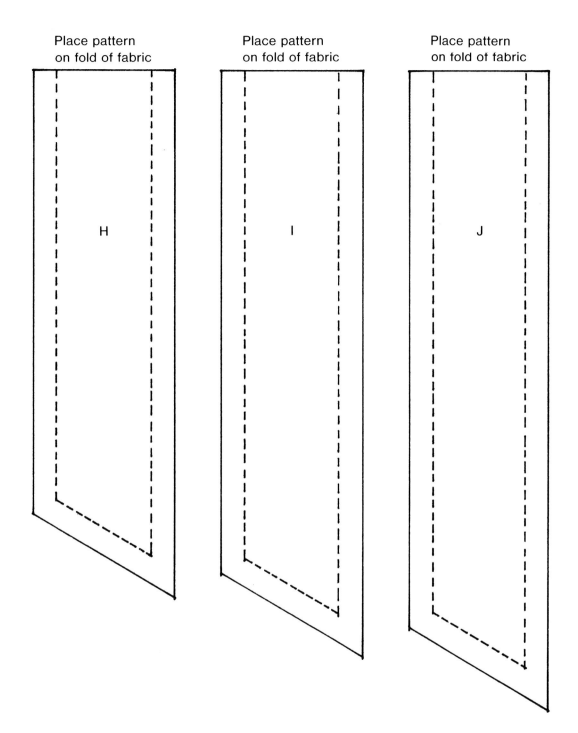

Triangle shaded diagram showing the use of block #1
and block #2

DIAMOND AND PARALLELOGRAM

Both the diamond and the parallelogram are cut from one versatile set of patterns with many possible arrangements. A simple yet effective design is the Alternating Diamond. For block #1 cut A in one light fabric. Cut two each from D and E in a second light fabric. Cut two each of H and I in a third light fabric. Cut two each of B and C in one dark fabric. Cut two each of F and G in a second dark fabric. For block #2 cut A in one dark fabric. Cut two each of D and E in a second dark fabric. Cut two each of H and I in a third dark fabric. Cut two each of B and C in one light fabric. Cut two each of F and G in a second light fabric.

Lay the B pieces right sides together on opposite sides of the A center piece, pin the seam lines together, and stitch. Press the seams away from the center. Join the C pieces on opposite sides of the center A piece and press the seams away from the center. Continue to join the pieces on opposite sides in alphabetical order, pressing the seams after each stitching.

The blocks must be joined in diagonal rows as with the triangles. The side and end blocks must be cut in half and the other half used on the opposite sides and ends. It is necessary to make a scaled diagram of the whole quilt plan to establish the number of blocks and rows needed.

Use the same fabric arrangement for both the parallelogram and the diamond version of the rectangle, changing fabrics for a two-block arrangement or using scrap fabric. Cut A in dark fabric. Cut two each of C, E, G, and I in dark fabrics. Cut two each of B, D, F, and H in light fabrics. Assemble the blocks alphabetically, as before. Use the shaded diagrams as a guide to joining the blocks to create the rectangular white areas.

For both the Diamond Star and the Tumbling Blocks make two different diamonds. For block #1 cut A in light fabric and all other pieces in dark fabric. For block #2 cut all pieces in light fabric. The fabrics may be mixed in any way, but the darks must contrast strongly with the lights. Use the shaded diagrams as a guide to joining the blocks. Each design is a large hexagon. The hexagons must then be joined as described on page 97 to form a whole quilt.

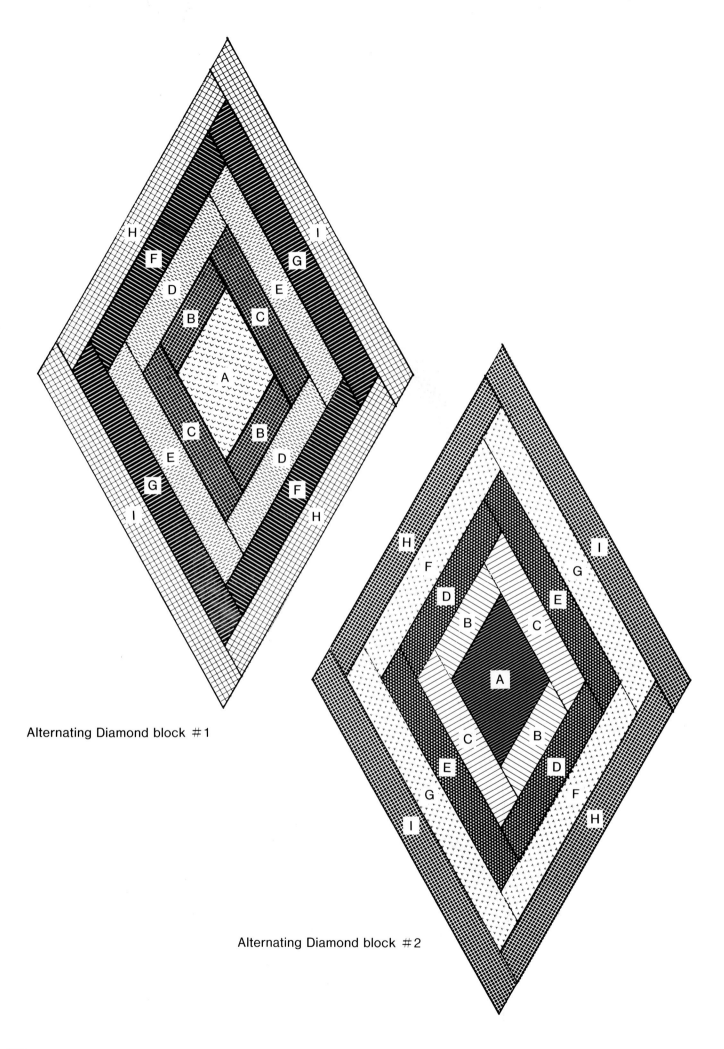

Alternating Diamond block #1

Alternating Diamond block #2

110

Parallelogram and Diamond piecing diagram

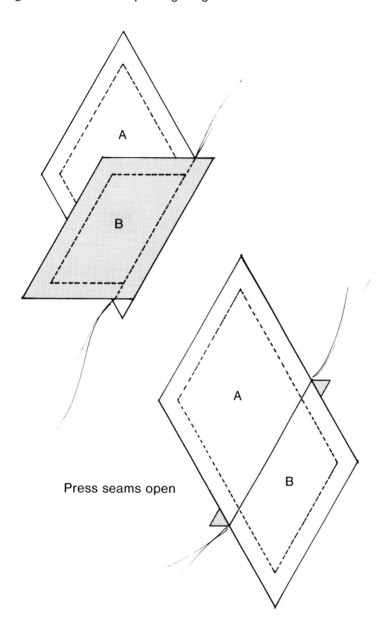

Press seams open

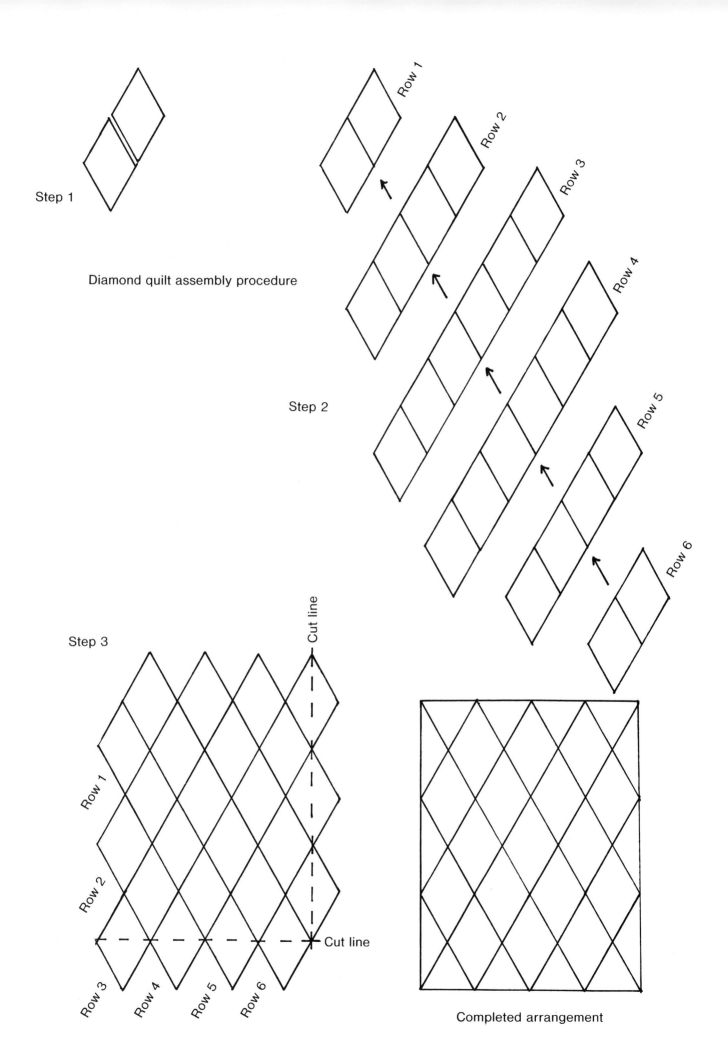

Step 1

Diamond quilt assembly procedure

Row 1

Row 2

Row 3

Row 4

Row 5

Row 6

Step 2

Step 3

Cut line

Row 1

Row 2

Cut line

Row 3   Row 4   Row 5   Row 6

Completed arrangement

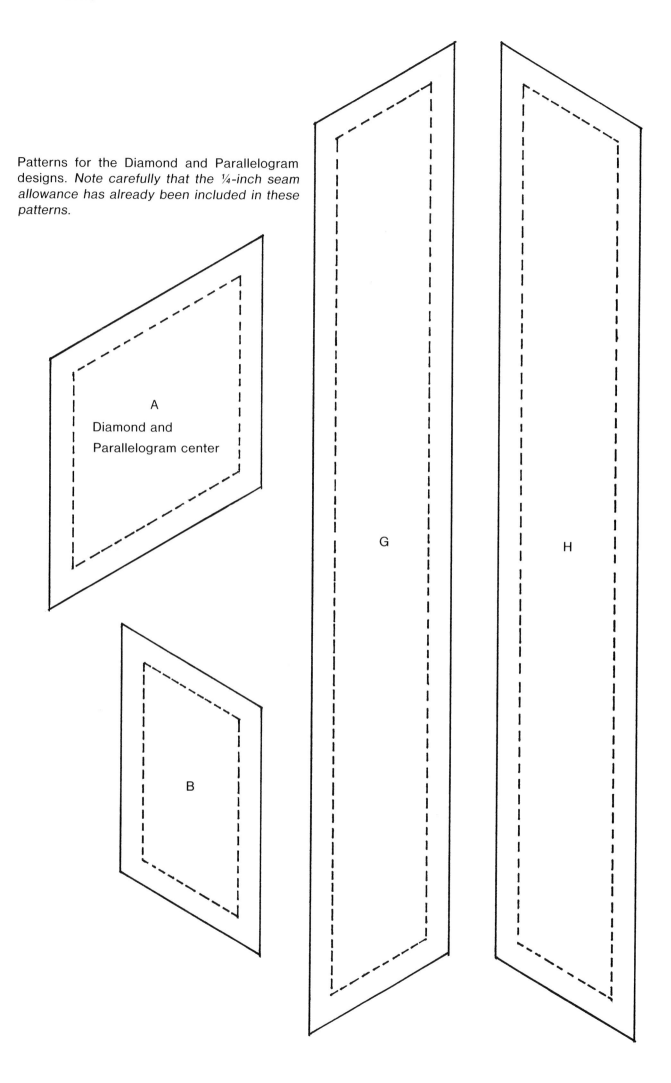

Patterns for the Diamond and Parallelogram designs. *Note carefully that the ¼-inch seam allowance has already been included in these patterns.*

A

Diamond and
Parallelogram center

B

G

H

113

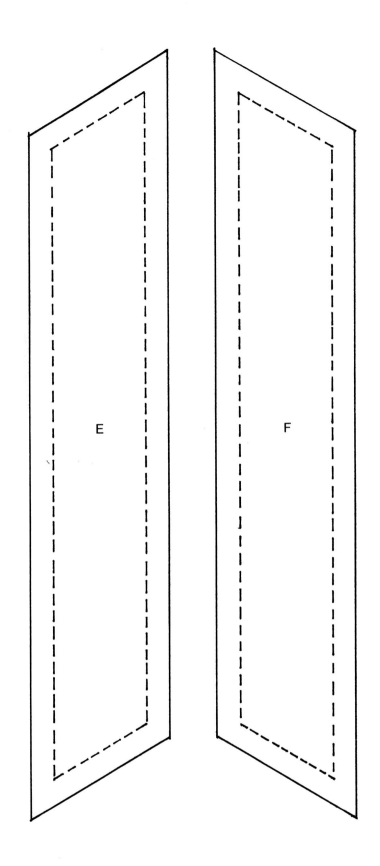

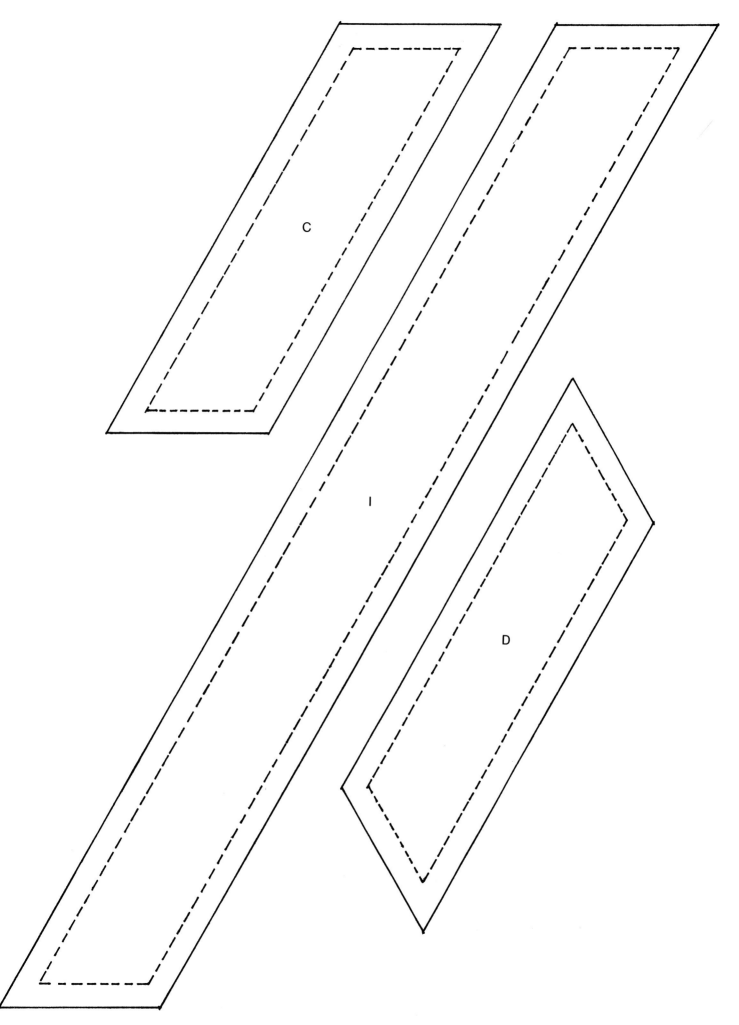

C

I

D

115

Alternating Diamond shaded diagram showing the arrangement of the blocks

Opposing light and dark Diamond or Parallelogram

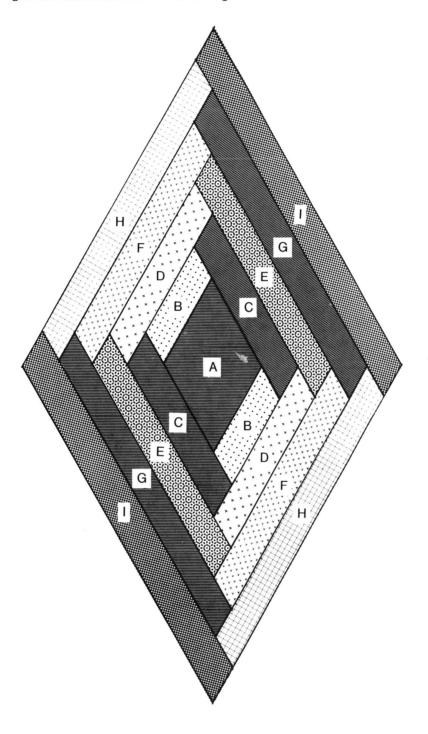

Diamond shaded diagram showing a rectangular formation
created by the light portion of the blocks

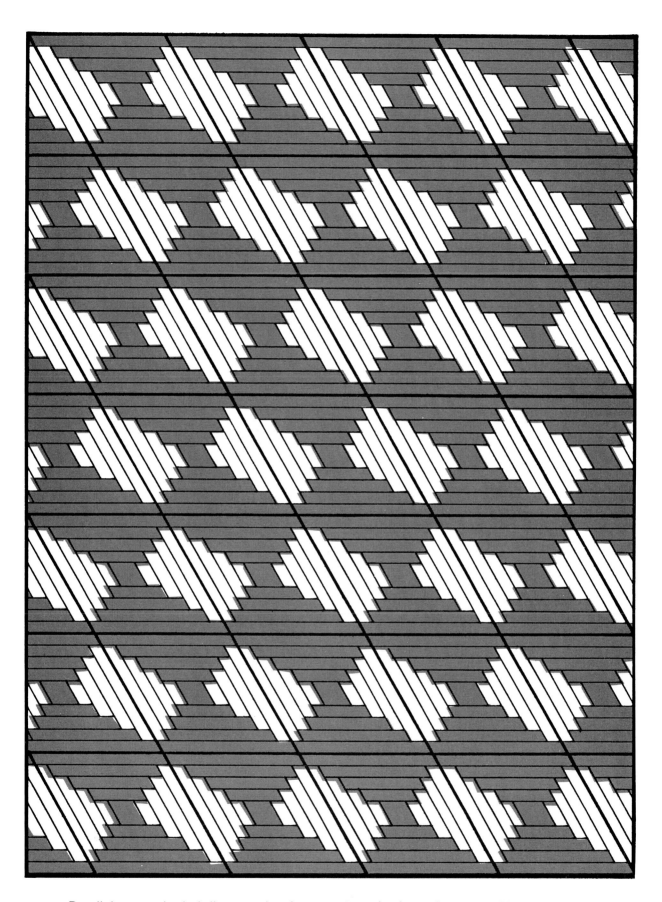

Parallelogram shaded diagram showing a rectangular formation created by the light portion of the blocks

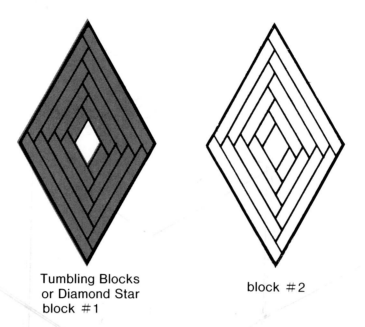

Tumbling Blocks
or Diamond Star
block #1

block #2

Tumbling Blocks shaded diagram of an arrangement of
light and dark Diamond blocks

Satin
in 3 shades
of three colors w/gold

Diamond Star shaded diagram of an arrangement of
light and dark Diamond blocks

OFF-CENTER LOG CABIN

Optical illusion is half the fun of any Log Cabin, and especially this one which creates curves from perfectly straight pieces. The increases in size of the total quilt or hanging must be made in increments of two blocks in each direction. They may be added one each to sides and ends or two to one side and two to one end.

Use either a two-block system or scrap pieces to prevent the identical long "logs" meeting at the focal points. For both blocks, if you use the two-block system, cut A in a dark fabric. Cut D and E in another dark fabric. Cut H and I in a third dark fabric, L and M in a fourth dark, P and Q in a fifth, T and U in a sixth, and X and Y in a seventh. Cut B and C of one light fabric, F and G in a second, J and K in a third, N and O in a fourth, R and S in a fifth, and V and W in a sixth. Assemble the pieces alphabetically, according to the diagram.

The design shown is only one of several that can be made by joining the blocks in varying arrangements. After you have made several blocks, lay them out to see what other optical illusions you can create.

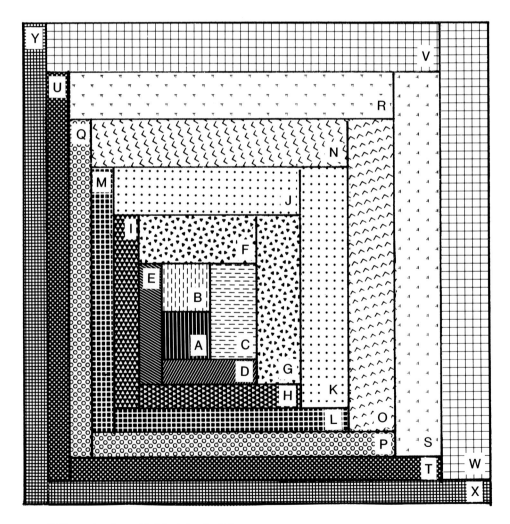

Off-center Log Cabin block #1

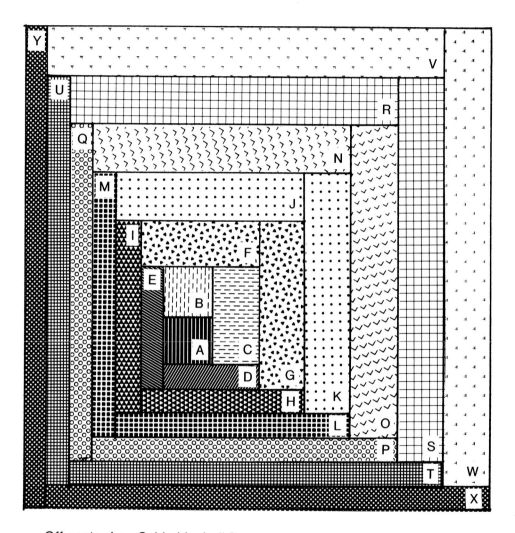

Off-center Log Cabin block #2

Patterns for the off-center Log Cabin design. *Note carefully that the ¼-inch seam allowance has already been included in these patterns.*

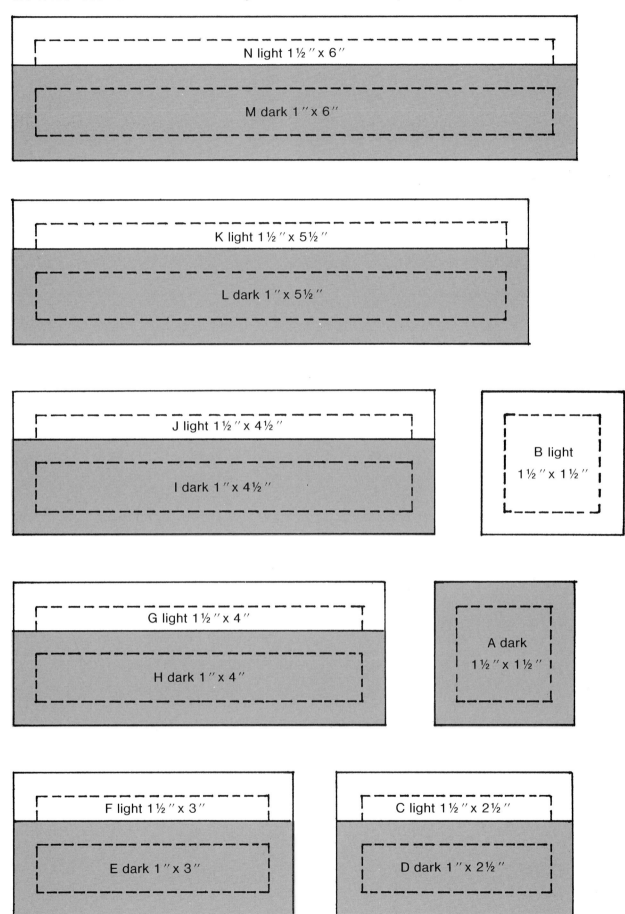

N light 1½″ x 6″

M dark 1″ x 6″

K light 1½″ x 5½″

L dark 1″ x 5½″

J light 1½″ x 4½″

I dark 1″ x 4½″

B light 1½″ x 1½″

G light 1½″ x 4″

H dark 1″ x 4″

A dark 1½″ x 1½″

F light 1½″ x 3″

E dark 1″ x 3″

C light 1½″ x 2½″

D dark 1″ x 2½″

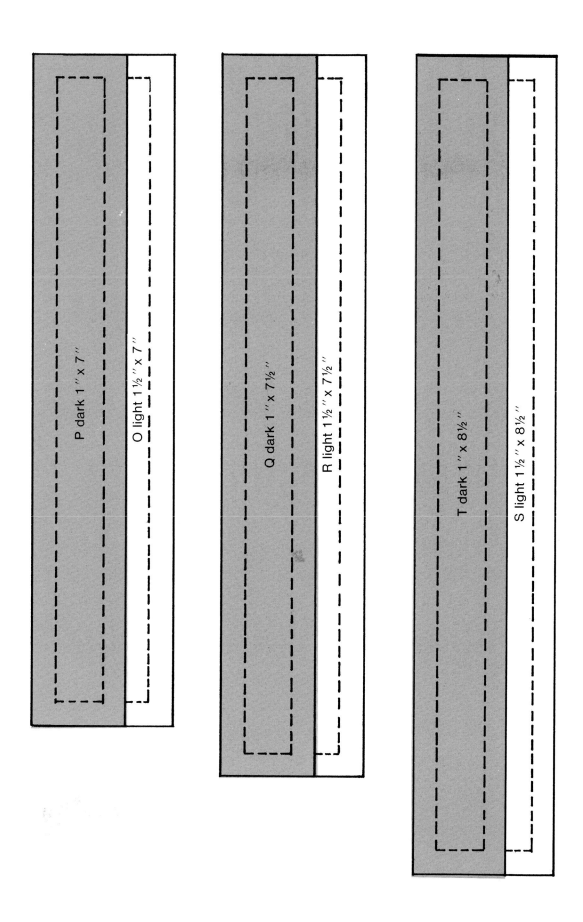

P dark 1" x 7"

O light 1½" x 7"

Q dark 1" x 7½"

R light 1½" x 7½"

T dark 1" x 8½"

S light 1½" x 8½"

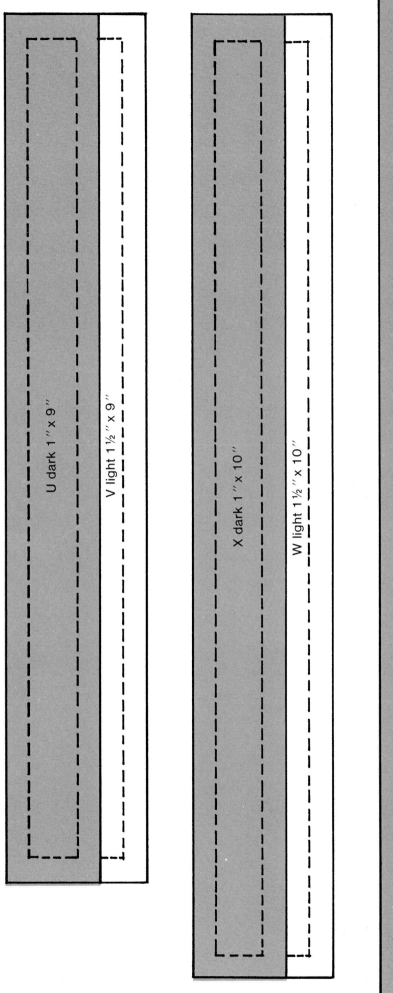

U dark 1″ x 9″

V light 1½″ x 9″

X dark 1″ x 10″

W light 1½″ x 10″

Y dark 1″ x 10½″

Off-center shaded diagram with narrow "logs" meeting

Off-center shaded diagram with wide "logs" meeting

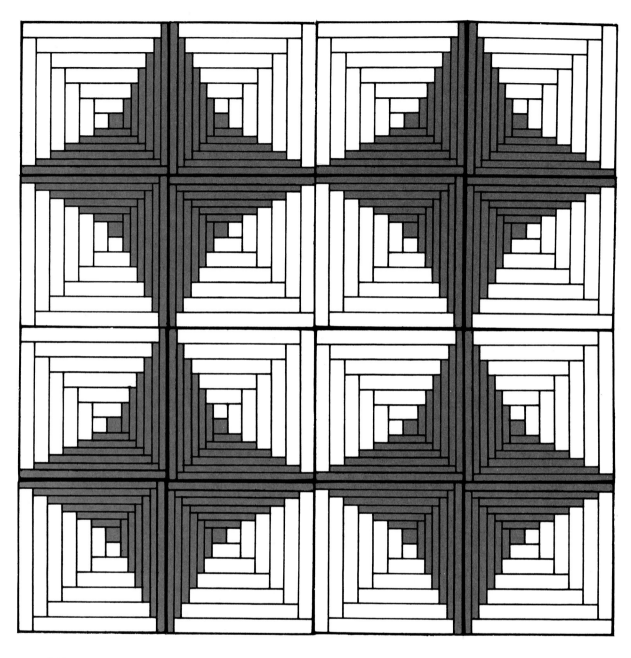

Off-center Log Cabin shaded diagram showing an arrangement of blocks creating a
curved effect

One Block at a Time or Quilt-as-You-Go

MAKING THE BLOCKS

Log Cabin designs are particularly suited to the Quilt-as-You-Go method of piecing. Each block is completed in a one-step operation, piecing, batting, and backing all stitched together. The completed blocks can then be joined to make a whole quilt that will need little or no more quilting. Only a binding is needed to finish the edges.

Use the backing fabric to make a foundation block 1 inch larger than the completed block size—9 inches for the basic 8-inch blocks, 11 inches for the Courthouse and White House Steps blocks, and 15 inches for the Pineapple. Fold the foundation blocks in half diagonally from corner to corner to find the center and crease along the lines to mark.

Cut batting blocks to the same size as the foundation blocks. Lay one foundation block right side down and pin a batting block to it, matching the sides evenly. Turn the blocks over so that you can see the creased lines in the foundation block, and baste the two layers together along these lines. Remove the pins.

Lay the piece of fabric cut from the A pattern piece in place wrong side down on the batting. Except in the Touching Stars and Chevron patterns, the A piece lies directly on the center of the block. Baste that first piece in place, working through all the layers. If you are skilled at pin basting and use the fine silk pins, you may be able to work with pins only and avoid the basting step. Lay the next (B) piece right side down on the A piece so that the raw edges are together, and stitch it into place as you would in the regular block-piecing procedure. Continue around the block, using the diagonal basting lines as a guide to keep the piece absolutely square (see order of assembly, steps 1 through 5).

On the final seams that run out to the raw edges, stop stitching ½ inch before the end of the seam and fasten the stitching with a backstitch. Join the remaining ½ inch through only the fabric layers of the "logs" by hand (Fig. 80). If you are piecing the entire block by hand, you do not need to fasten off the thread at the ½-inch point but can bring the needle up to the surface and work through only the two layers to the end. By leaving the backing free for this ½ inch, you will make the joining of the blocks and the finishing much neater.

Press Piecing order of assembly

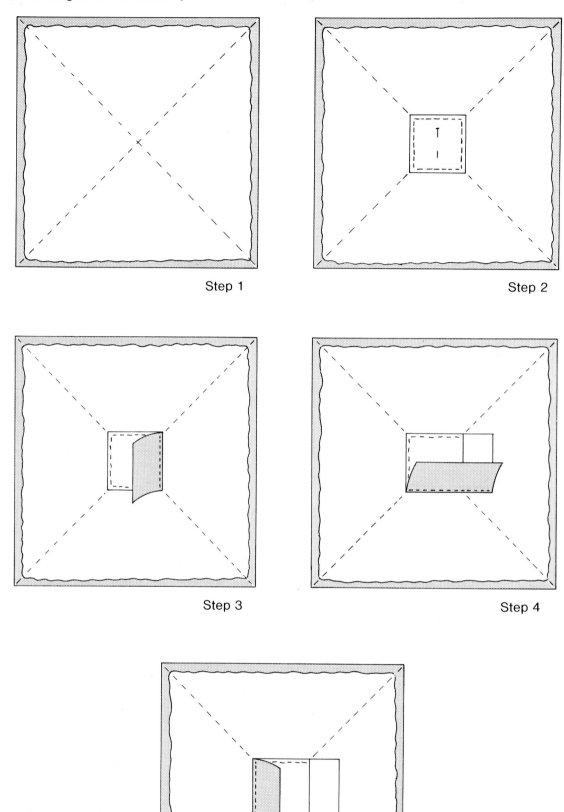

Step 1

Step 2

Step 3

Step 4

Step 5

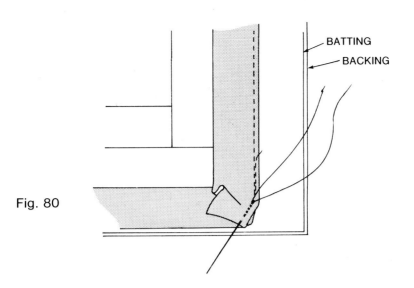

BATTING

BACKING

Fig. 80

JOINING THE BLOCKS
AND FINISHING THE BACKING

Trim the batting and backing even with the block top. Lay the blocks out in order, as described in Chapter IV. Pick up the first two blocks and lay them right sides together. Pin through the top and batting, but fold the backing out of the way. Stitch along the ¼-inch seamline. Trim the batting close to the stitching (Fig. 81).

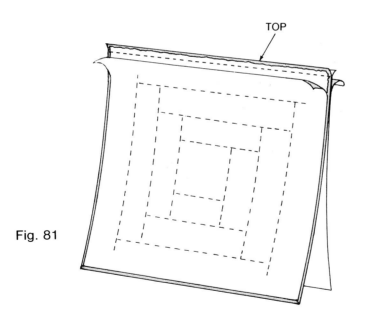

TOP

Fig. 81

Continue piecing together the blocks until one row is completed. The seams may be pressed to one side or open flat. If they are pressed to one side, alternate the direction on adjoining rows so that the corners will be less bulky when the rows are seamed together (see Chapter IV).

The backing must be finished on each row before the rows are joined together. Lay the pressed row of blocks right side down on a table. Smooth the backing flat and pin it, working on one edge of each block, all the way along the row, so that the other edge of each block is still free. Turn under that loose edge ¼ inch and pin it smoothly over the flat edge (Fig. 82). The turned edge should lie directly over the seamline that joins the two blocks. Use a blindstitch to finish the folded edge, leaving it loose ½ inch from each end so that the rows may be seamed together in the same way (Fig. 83). Finish the quilt by seaming the long rows together, trimming the batting, and turning under the loose edge for blindstitching.

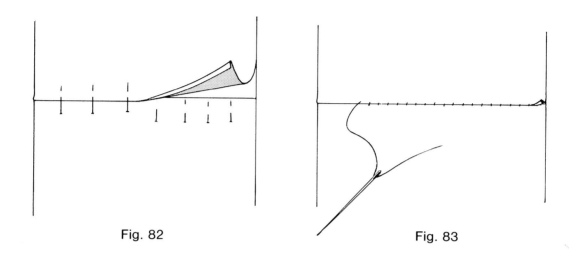

Fig. 82   Fig. 83

The back of the finished quilt will look almost as though it had been quilted, by machine or hand, depending upon your method of attaching the "logs" to the foundation blocks. On the right side no stitches will show, but there will be an indentation along each seamline as in the "stitch-in-the-ditch" method of quilting (page 39). If you have kept all the seaming very even and stopped exactly ½ inch from the ends of the last seams, you may not feel the need to finish the small ¼-inch space of stitching at the ends of those last "logs."

The long seamline that joins blocks and the even longer one that joins rows can be improved by quilting through all the layers. If the quilt is quite large, it will probably be necessary to do the quilting by hand, with a needle slightly heavier than usual. On a smaller piece you may be able to stitch by machine, rolling the quilt tightly from each side to fit under the machine head.

Quilt Care

WASHING AND CLEANING

Sooner or later most cotton quilts will need to be washed. That's a big job, no matter how you go about it, and the ways of doing it change as fast as new washing methods are invented. Only a few years ago washing machines were manual affairs that beat fabrics and ran them through wringers. Now we have washers with gentle cycles, kind enough for our daintiest lingerie.

Old-fashioned yellow soap has gone the way of the mangle and the wringer, and there are now a whole battery of liquid detergents made especially for delicate fabrics. If you have taken precautions as described in Chapter II, and have preshrunk and color-tested all your fabrics, a strong new quilt can be washed in a machine far more easily than by hand—and with better results.

If there are spots on the quilt that are difficult to remove, you may pretreat them by rubbing the liquid detergent directly on them with a soft cloth or a cotton swab for very small spots. Ensure, made especially for quilts, is very good, as are Miracle White liquid and New Improved Era. Use any of these detergents as directed on the bottle. The water in the machine should be cool. Spray and Wash is another safe pretreatment to be used before immersing the quilt in the washer.

Spread the quilt around the center agitator in the machine so that the weight is evenly distributed. After the water has run, stop the machine cycle so that the quilt simply soaks in the water and detergent. When you are satisfied that it has soaked long enough, let the wash water run out and the rinse water run in. When the rinse water has run out, stop the machine action and rearrange the quilt so that it is loose and does not touch the central agitator. Let it spin and rinse again and repeat the process.

The secret of machine washing a quilt is to use plenty of water, at least two rinses, and as little twisting and pulling as possible. Many people have said that quilts should be washed by hand, but it is almost impossible to do this under ordinary household conditions without pulling on and twisting the quilt enough to break threads or even tear the fabric. If you do plan to wash an antique quilt at home, be sure that you have a large enough tub and someone to help you lift and move the quilt—very gently.

HANGING A QUILT

Quilts are often hung in shows, and there are usually specific requirements in each show as to the method of hanging; in general a good "sleeve" sewed onto the back of the quilt at the top edge will do the trick. If you plan to hang a quilt as a wall decoration, you can also use a sleeve.

Cut a strip of muslin about 7 inches wide and as long as the width of the quilt. Fold it in half lengthwise, right sides together, and stitch a ¼-inch seam around the ends and the long raw edge, leaving a small opening for turning (Fig. 84). Cut off the corners and turn the tube right side out. Blind-stitch the opening closed and press the tube flat (Fig. 85).

Fig. 84

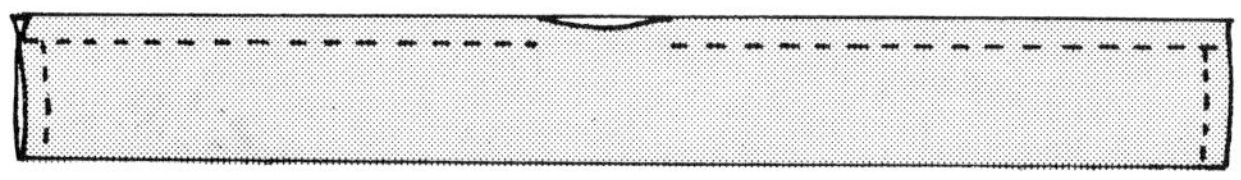

Fig. 85

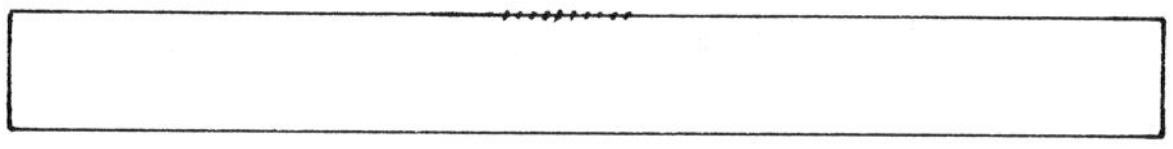

Using a strong thread or a double thread, whip-stitch the upper and lower edges of the tube to the top of the back of the quilt, about an inch down from the edge (Fig. 86). A metal rod or smooth wooden slat can be run through the sleeve and suspended by wires. For a more permanent installation you may want to turn the corners of the quilt back out of the way and tack the ends of the wooden slat to the wall.

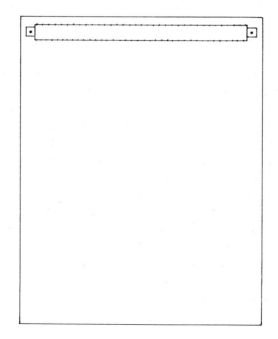

Fig. 86

For a permanent hanging you may want to add another sleeve at the lower edge of the quilt so that a second slat or rod can be installed as a weight to hold the piece smooth and flat. The wood slats used in long-term installations should be sealed with a clear shellac to prevent discoloration of the fabric.

Strips of Velcro® can be used along the upper edge—or upper and lower edges—of wall hangings. The other piece of Velcro® is then attached to a wood frame or to a molding, using any good glue such as Sobo®. The cost of Velcro® makes this fairly prohibitive for any but small pieces, but the method is especially good for odd-shaped hangings—hexagons or other pieces that need a frame all around.

PACKING AND SHIPPING A QUILT

You may have heard or read long discussions of the problems of packing quilts away in storage and of shipping them safely. Most of these discussions are dealing with valuable and fragile antiques. For our purposes, dealing with your newly made, sturdy Log Cabin quilt, a little common sense is the best equipment.

If you want to put your quilt away for the summer, be sure it is clean. Spots tend to become more permanent the longer they stay in. A large suit box lined with white tissue paper is suitable for short-term storage. A clean white pillowcase can be used as a container and will take up less room on the linen closet shelf than a box. Never store a quilt where the sun or the rain may get to it, or where the family pet will find what a great bed it makes.

We all think our quilts are extremely valuable, but overinsuring is just as bad as not insuring at all when you ship one to a friend or to a show. Try to get a realistic perspective on the value by looking at similar quilts in shops or by asking several quilt "experts" such as teachers, shop owners, and collectors.

There are many good, reliable shipping companies, but any shipper is only as good as the packing that comes to the truck. The U.S. Postal Service, for all its slow delivery, does a very good job with registered mail and will insure for a reasonably high figure. There are very set rules for the packing of registered mail—get the list *before* you start.

Use a good, strong corrugated box and proper package tape, no matter which shipper you choose. Put the quilt in a clean cloth bag (that old pillowcase again) and then in a plastic bag inside the box. You have now guarded against water damage and damage caused by the package being laid against a radiator so hot that the plastic melts onto the quilt—both only slight possibilities but known to have happened. Be sure to include an address card inside the box as well as a clearly typed or printed label outside. If the quilt is to be returned to you, ask that the same care be taken.

Bibliography

Aylsworth, Susan, and Payne, Suzy Chalfant. *Quick and Easy Patchwork on the Sewing Machine.* New York: Dover Publications, Inc., 1979.

Bacon, Lenice. *American Patchwork Quilts.* New York: William Morrow & Co., Inc., 1973.

Beyer, Jinny. *Patchwork Patterns.* McLean, Virginia: EPM Publications, 1979.

Bishop, Robert, and Safanda, Elizabeth. *A Gallery of Amish Quilts.* New York: E. P. Dutton, Inc., 1976.

Bishop, Robert. *New Discoveries in American Quilts.* New York: E. P. Dutton, Inc., 1975.

Brown, Elsa. *Creative Quilting.* New York: Watson-Guptill Publications, 1975.

Colby, Averil. *Patchwork.* London: B. T. Batsford, Ltd., 1958.

Cooper, Patricia, and Bufferd, Norma. *The Quilters.* New York: Doubleday & Co., Inc., 1977.

Cox, Patricia. *The Log Cabin Workbook.* Minneapolis, Minnesota: One of a Kind Quilting Designs, 1980.

Danneman, Barbara. *Step by Step Quiltmaking.* New York: Golden Press, 1975.

Dittrick, Mark, and Morrow, Susan. *Patchwork Plain and Fancy.* New York: Berkley Publishing Corporation, 1973.

Echols, Margit. *The Quilter's Coloring Book.* New York: Thomas Y. Crowell Publishers, 1979.

Finley, Ruth. *Old Patchwork Quilts and the Women Who Made Them.* Philadelphia: J. B. Lippincott, 1946.

Frager, Dorothy. *The Quilting Primer.* Radnor, Pennsylvania: Chilton Book Company, 1974.

Gammell, Alice I. *Polly Prindle's Book of American Patchwork.* New York: Grossett & Dunlap, Inc., 1973.

Gutcheon, Beth. *The Perfect Patchwork Primer.* New York: David McKay Co., Inc., 1973.

Gutcheon, Beth and Jeffrey. *Quilt Design Workbook.* New York: Rawson Associates Publishers, Inc., 1976.

Haders, Phyllis. *Sunshine and Shadow: The Amish and Their Quilts.* New York: The Main Street Press, 1976.

Hall, Carrie A., and Kretsinger, Rose G. *The Romance of the Patchwork Quilt in America.* New York: Bonanza Books, 1935.

Hassel, Carla J. *Super Quilter II.* Des Moines, Iowa: Wallace-Homestead Book Company, 1982.

Heard, Audrey, and Pryor, Beverly. *Complete Guide to Quilting.* Des Moines, Iowa: Meredith Corporation, 1974.

Hinson, Dolores. *Quilting Manual.* Knoxville, Tennessee: Hearthside Press, Inc., 1970.

Holstein, Jonathan. *The Pieced Quilt: An American Tradition.* Greenwich, Connecticut: New York Graphic Society, 1973.

Houck, Carter, and Miller, Myron. *American Quilts and How to Make Them.* New York: Charles Scribner's Sons, 1975.

Ickis, Margaret. *The Standard Book of Quiltmaking.* New York: Dover Publications, 1959.

James, Michael. *The Quiltmaker's Handbook.* Englewood Cliffs, New Jersey: Prentice-Hall, Inc., 1978.

————. *The Second Quiltmaker's Handbook.* Englewood Cliffs, New Jersey: Prentice-Hall, Inc., 1981.

Johannah, Barbara. *The Quick Quiltmaking*

Handbook. Menlo Park, California: Pride of the Forest Press, 1979.

Johnson, Bruce. *A Child's Comfort.* New York: Harcourt Brace Jovanovich, 1977.

Larsen, Judith LaBelle, and Gull, Carol Waugh. *The Patchwork Quilt Design and Coloring Book.* New York: Butterick Publishing, 1977.

Laury, Jean Ray. *Quilts and Coverlets: A Contemporary Approach.* New York: Van Nostrand Reinhold Co., 1970.

Leman, Bonnie, and Martin, Judy. *Log Cabin Quilts.* Wheatridge, Colorado: Moon Over the Mountain Publishing Company, 1980.

Lewis, Alfred Allan. *The Mountain Artisans' Quilting Book.* New York: Macmillan Co., Inc., 1973.

Mahler, Celine. *Once Upon a Quilt.* New York: Van Nostrand Reinhold Co., 1973.

Orlofsky, Patsy and Myron. *Quilts in America.* New York: McGraw-Hill Book Company, 1974.

Pforr, Effie. *Award Winning Quilts.* Birmingham, Alabama: Oxmoor House, Inc., 1974.

Rose, Helen Whitson. *Quilting with Strips and Strings.* New York: Dover Publications, Inc., 1983.

Safford, Carleton L., and Bishop, Robert. *America's Quilts and Coverlets.* New York: E. P. Dutton, Inc., 1972.

Shogren, Linda. *The Log Cabin Compendium.* San Mateo, California: Linda Shogren Quilting Publications, 1977.

Wilson, Erica. *Quilts of America.* Birmingham, Alabama: Oxmoor House, Inc., 1979.

Woodard, Thomas, and Greenstein, Blanche. *Crib Quilts and Other Small Wonders.* New York: E. P. Dutton, Inc., 1981.

Woodster, Ann-Sargent. *Quiltmaking.* New York: Drake Publishers, Inc., 1972.

Sources

Suggested mail-order sources for quilting supplies, templates, books, and patterns:

Quilts & Other Comforts
Box 394
Wheatridge, Colorado   80033

Cabin Fever Calicoes
Box 6256
Washington, D.C.   20015

Ginger Snap Station
P.O. Box 81086
Atlanta, Georgia   30341

Mrs. Wigg's Cabbage Patch, Inc.
2600 Beaver Avenue
Des Moines, Iowa   50310

The Silver Thimble
249 High Street
Ipswich, Massachusetts   01938

The Quiltworks
216 Third Avenue N.
Minneapolis, Minnesota   55401

Country Peddler
2242 Carter Avenue
St. Paul, Minnesota   55108

Glad Creations
3400 Bloomington Avenue
South Minneapolis, Minnesota   55407

Quilt Country
500 Nichols Road
Kansas City, Missouri   64112

Mail-in
P.O. Box 157
Schroon Lake, New York   12870

Gutcheon Patchworks
611 Broadway
New York, New York   10012

Cross Patch
Rt. #9
Garrison, New York   10524

Creative Quilt Center
Stearns & Foster
Box 15380
Cincinnati, Ohio   45215

Great Expectations
155 Town and Country Village
Houston, Texas   77024

Let's Quilt and Sew-on
P.O. Box 29526
San Antonio, Texas   78229

Calico Country Store
10822 124th Street
Edmonton, Alberta
Canada   T5M 0H3

Suggested books for beginners:

The Perfect Patchwork Primer
by Beth Gutcheon
David McKay Company, Inc.
750 3rd Avenue
New York, New York   10017

Quick and Easy Quilting
by Bonnie Leman
Moon Over the Mountain Publishing
  Company
6700 West 44th Avenue
Wheatridge, Colorado   80033

You Can Be a Super Quilter
by Carla Hassel
Wallace-Homestead Book Company
1912 Grand Avenue
Des Moines, Iowa   50305

Carol Anne Wien studied art at Syracuse University and at the Art Students League, and received a degree in Fine Arts from the University of Miami. She did postgraduate work at Georgia State University and the University of Miami, where she taught quiltmaking for seven years through the Continunig Education Program. She has lectured widely, exhibited her quilts in solo and group shows, and has won national awards for several of her quilts. Her works are in many private collections.

In 1982 Mrs. Wien was co-chairman of one of the largest cultural series in south Florida, and she has been involved in numerous charitable and civic organizations through the years. Carol lives in Miami, Florida, with her husband and two children.